Waiting for Boaz

Encouragement for women desiring
marriage God's way

Obieray Rogers

Forward by Bishop Timothy J. Clarke

This work is dedicated to my son, Quentin, for his unconditional love and steadfast belief that his mother can do anything.

To my grandsons, Quentin and Quency, who are Boazes in the making.

And to all of my sisters in the Lord who have chosen to wait for Boaz.

Acknowledgments

I am always amazed by God's sovereignty. Only He knows why He gives certain project to certain people. I am thankful that He trusted me enough with this work, and I freely give Him all the praise and honor.

I am grateful...

To the people God has placed in my life that believed, encouraged and supported this effort, especially my family, friends and acquaintances...

To my spiritual covering, Bishop Timothy J. Clarke and First Lady, "Sister C," for their unwavering support and prayers...

To the Maieutics: those who pushed, prodded and provoked me to finish this work. They unselfishly offered their time, support, prayers, laughter and tears, and together we made it...

And to you for reading this work. I pray that you will be blessed.

Foreword

One of my favorite sayings is one that I do not know the origin or the author of, but I have lived its message and understand the meaning: "Who taught you how to pray? Trouble taught me how to pray! Who taught you how to sing? Sorrow taught me how to sing!" As I read the pages of this book I could not help but ask, "Who taught you how to write?" and the answer could well be, "Pain taught me how to write!"

I am convinced that all of us have music and poetry within us, but seldom do we let it out or allow it to find expression. How grateful we all should be that Obie Rogers has found her voice and released through her pen that which dwells within her. If you know her, then you know she is a no-holds barred, tell-it-like-it-is kind of person and in this book she writes the way she lives.

Some people need to say something, and some have something that needs to be said. What is in this book needs to be said. Here is a hard-hitting treatment of relationships in real life. Obie not only shows us how it is, but she shows us the possibility of how it can and should be.

I suppose that what makes this book so powerful is that it is written with experience and compassion. I know that as you read it you will be blessed, challenged and helped.

Bishop Timothy J. Clarke, Senior Pastor
First Church of God, Columbus, Ohio

Table of Contents

I once overheard a conversation between two Christian women, one of whom was married. It was the type of conversation where a number of people were talking at the same time and you tuned in when something caught your attention. The married woman had evidently said something to the single woman about not taking just any man that came along. The single woman responded with, "Girl, you don't have to worry. I'm waiting on my Boaz!" Although I was familiar with the story of Ruth and Boaz I had never heard a response like that but remembered thinking, "Me, too!"

If you are not familiar with the story of Ruth and Boaz, here's a very brief synopsis. A more detailed overview of the book of Ruth follows this introduction. Ruth was a Moabitess who moved back to Bethlehem, Judah with her mother-in-law, Naomi, after the death of her husband, Mahlon. She arrived at the beginning of the barley harvest season and sought work in the field of the richest man in the area: A man named Boaz. After working through both the barley and wheat harvests, Naomi devised a plan whereby Ruth asked Boaz to fulfill his family obligation. Boaz agreed and they married. They had a son named Obed who would be King David's great-grandfather.

One of the wonderful benefits of being a Christian is having God order your steps and direct your path. I know that a part of God's plan for my life includes marriage. And once God gave me His Word, I began to prepare by seeking

Him for direction. When I also began to make note of the attributes I would like my husband to personify, Boaz always came to mind. Every time I read the book of Ruth, there are qualities about Boaz that literally jump off the page. I am convinced that Boaz—a whole and complete person—is the type of man every Christian woman who desires marriage should be waiting for. Simply put, Boaz is God's choice for you.

Waiting for Boaz is not a how-to-catch-a-man of type book, but it is a how-to-wait-for-God's-choice type of book. God has inspired me to share thoughts, ideas and concepts with you based on my experiences and observations and the insight God has given me.

Let me caution you that parts of this book won't make sense if you do not have a personal relationship with the Lord Jesus Christ. If that is the case, today is the perfect day to give your life to the Lord. God wants you more than you could ever want Him, and He is waiting to give you what you need to make it through this journey called life.

You may be wondering why God would give me this book. Actually, that is the same question I asked God and He gave me three reasons:

- God knows I have a strong desire to see His women walking in what He has for them. Second best isn't good enough.

- I have a burden for single people, especially women. I am living proof that single women are just as blessed and highly favored as married women, although society and the church will sometimes try to convince you otherwise. Single women are neither inferior nor forgotten by God, although some women act that way. If I can get just one woman to read this book and reconsider settling for less than God's best, then *Waiting for Boaz* will have accomplished its purpose.

- God knows I will be honest and truthful. In the fore-word, Bishop Clarke referred to me as a no-holds barred type of person, which has advantages and dis-advantages. The advantage is that people never have to worry about what I meant by what was said. The disadvantage is that some people prefer their truth sugar coated and not so "in your face." The reality is that all of us have within us things that need to be shared in our voice in order to bless others. *Waiting for Boaz* is my contribution to God's women. I am single, I am saved and I am waiting. Not twiddling my thumbs waiting, but waiting with a sense of anticipa-tion about whom, when and where. I can share my experiences with you and realize that we are probably a lot alike. Besides, aren't you tired of married women telling you to "just hold on, honey," while they go home to their husbands every night? When they turn over in bed, they bump into their man; when I turn over, I bump into my extra pillows!

I also believe that God gave me this book to correct at least two societal myths.

MYTH NUMBER ONE:

If you are a certain age and still single, there must be something wrong with you.

There is nothing wrong with being single, and just because you haven't married does not mean that you are too picky or gay. It could mean that you have chosen to wait for God's choice instead of giving into your flesh.

Being single allows you the opportunity to do things you won't be able to do once you are married and/or have children. Right now you can be as selfish as you like when it comes to the things of God in the sense of praying as long as you want, fasting when you feel led (without having to explain) and spending as much time with God as you desire. All of these are excellent spiritual advantages of being single.

There are also other advantages like traveling or trying new careers. You have the freedom to come and go as you please, and there is no one you have to be accountable to although you should certainly be accountable to someone. My point is that if you want to go out after work, you probably don't have to call home and explain. If you want to buy something new, you don't have to get into a long debate about it (providing you have the money and the Lord has released you to spend it). If something gets broke, you know you broke it; if something gets messed up, you know you did it and if you put something in the refrigerator, it is still there when you go back for it!

Singleness is not a disease and we need to stop acting like it is. We must guard against falling into the trap the enemy sets for us by feeling sorry for ourselves or letting other people feel sorry for us. If God has allowed you to be single, this is your most productive season:

> *An unmarried woman or virgin is concerned about the Lord's affairs. Her aim is to be devoted to the Lord in both body and spirit. But a married woman is concerned about the affairs of this world—how she can please her husband* (1 Corinthians 7:34).

This may not be one of your favorite Bible verses, but it is still true. There are things that you can do single that you will never be able to do either married or married with children. Get busy being about God's business while you have time.

MYTH NUMBER TWO:

A woman is not complete without a man.

Please! You are already a complete person.

Marriage will not make you whole, complete or happy. That can only be found in an intimate relationship with the Lord Jesus Christ. If you are not already whole, complete and happy going into marriage, you will be miserable and most likely will make your spouse (and everyone else) miserable, too.

People who embrace this myth are partly responsible for the divorce rate being so high. If your environment is one where this type of myth is constantly reinforced, i.e., from parents, church, co-workers and so on, then after a while you will jump on the first man who looks your way just to shut these people up. Is that smart? No. But it is the reality of some women. They marry inappropriately and when they have had all they can stand, divorce is the only option. It is really sad, especially when it comes from the church. Some churches are not teaching their women that they are already whole and complete; they are not second-class citizens standing on the periphery of life waiting for some man to bring them onto the stage. One is a whole number.

Recently within a three-hour period I watched TBN, BET Inspiration and the Word Channel. Within that three-hour period every preacher talked about single people waiting for the right person, getting in the right place to be blessed and so on. There was nothing wrong with anything they said because it was sound, biblical advice. But then one of the preachers made the statement that you don't became complete until you get married. Perhaps he meant to say that marriage complements you because if I am not complete until I get married, does that mean that those who never marry are incomplete? I don't think so:

For you created my inmost being; you knit me together in my mother's womb. I praise you because I am fearfully and wonderfully made; your works are wonderful, I know that full well. My frame was not hidden from you when I was made in the secret place. When I was woven together in the depths of the earth, your eyes saw my unformed body. All the days ordained for me were written in your book before one of them came to be (Psalm 139:13-16).

I believe marriage may fulfill some areas, but I am challenged by the word "complete" and prefer the word "complement." There are two ways to spell this one word and they have different meanings. Compliment means to flatter or praise; complement means to bring to perfection. That is what marriage does; it brings two complete and whole people who complement each other together.

God created singleness and marriage and both have a specific purpose. We are to master one before we move onto the next, and God is not going to change your marital status until you have accomplished all that you were supposed to while single. God gives you what you need when you need it, never before.

If you have been single for a while, there are probably habits so ingrained that it will take a bulldozer to break through. God knew that before he presented me with my Boaz He would have to work on some of my rough edges, and there were a lot. He has put men in my life who have taught me submission and accountability, although they weren't aware of how God was using them. Recently the Lord has placed men in my life to teach me another aspect of accountability by asking, "Where have you been?" type questions. I will admit that I failed the test several times before I realized I was even in a test. My original smart-mouth answer would have been, "None of your business" in a nice Christian way, of course. Now, no matter what smart remark surfaces, I allow the Lord to control my tongue (ouch!).

My point is that you need to take advantage of the men already in your life, whether family, friends or co-workers. You don't jump from single to married overnight. There is a period of preparation and usually that preparation occurs before your Boaz arrives on the scene. All of the men in your life are there for a reason and the reason may be to get you ready for marriage. Keep in mind that you don't get married to get ready; you get ready to get married.

The next time someone comes at you with either of the above myths, or any other one, I want you to look them in the eye and let them know you are a whole and complete woman and there is nothing wrong with you because you are single. Don't feel bad about it or apologize. God knows you better than you will ever know yourself and at His appointed time your marital status will change. And if it doesn't, God will help you deal with that, too. Whatever you do, don't jump ahead of God's timing.

The fact that you are reading this indicates a curiosity about marriage. There is a possibility that you may not agree with everything I have written, and that is okay. This book is what God has said to me. You may have to use your sanctified imagination to hear what God is saying to you.

If God has said marriage is for you, there is only one way to do it—His way! And His way means *Waiting for Boaz!*

Did you know that according to the Romance Writers of America, the romance industry generated $1.36 billion in sales in 2009? Did you know that the romance novel format is taken straight from the story of Ruth and Boaz? Think about it: Man notices woman (Ruth 2:5-6); man meets woman (Ruth 2:7); man and woman have numerous interactions (Ruth 2 and 3); man and woman have obstacles to overcome (Ruth 3:1, 12-13); man and woman marry and live happily ever after (Ruth 4:13). It is the classic romance novel scenario because:

> *That which has been is what will be, that which is done is what will be done, and there is nothing new under the sun* (Ecclesiastes 1:9, NKJV).

The story of Ruth and Boaz is one of the Bible's greatest love stories. It demonstrates God's love for humanity, man's love for a woman and our love for each other. This story has all the drama of a daytime soap or the page-turning intensity of a juicy mystery novel. There is suspense, intrigue, temptation, romance and a happy ending. Stories don't come any better than this.

Throughout the rest of this book we are going to examine closely some of the integral parts of this story, but here is a brief overview.

A man named Elimelech moved his family (wife Naomi and sons Mahlon and Kilion) from Bethlehem in Judah to Moab. While in Moab Elimelech died and his sons married Moabite women—Mahlon to Ruth and Kilion to Orpah. Eventually both sons died, and Naomi prepared to return to Bethlehem. She encouraged her daughters-in-law to return to their own families. Orpah stayed in Moab, but Ruth insisted on accompanying Naomi to Bethlehem.

Naomi and Ruth arrived in Bethlehem at the beginning of the barley harvest season (April), and Ruth sought work gleaning in a field that just happened to belong to Boaz, the richest man in the area. Gleaners were those people who came behind the reapers and were allowed to have whatever the reapers missed. The Law provided gleaning as a way of taking care of those less fortunate:

> *When you are harvesting in your field and you overlook a sheaf, do not go back to get it. Leave it for the alien, the fatherless and the widow, so that the Lord your God may bless you in all the work of your hands* (Deuteronomy 24:19).

Boaz noticed Ruth working in his field and offered his protection:

> *So Boaz said to Ruth, "My daughter, listen to me. Don't go and glean in another field and don't go away from here. Stay here with my servant girls. Watch the field where the men are harvesting, and follow along after the girls. I have told the men not to touch you. And whenever you are thirsty, go and get a drink from the water jars the men have filled* (Ruth 2:8-9).

When Ruth wondered why Boaz was being so nice to her, he said it was because he had heard how she had left her home and family to return with Naomi and of all the good things she had done for her mother-in-law (Ruth 2:11).

Ruth returned home from her first day of work with leftover lunch and the grain she had gleaned. It was so much more than would have normally been gleaned—approximately twenty-eight pounds—that Naomi (wanting to know who had shown her such kindness) asked, *"Where did you glean today? Where did you work? Blessed be the man who took notice of you!"* (Ruth 2:19a). Ruth told her that she had met Boaz and shared all that he had said and done. Naomi explained that Boaz was the family's kinsman redeemer via Elimelech. According to custom, a kinsman redeemer was expected to do one or all of the following:

- Buy back family land that had been sold (Leviticus 25:25).
- Look after needy and helpless family members (Leviticus 25:35).
- Buy back family members sold into slavery (Leviticus 25:47-49).
- Avenge the death of a murdered relative (Numbers 35:19).
- Marry a childless widow (Deuteronomy 25:5-10).

Ruth worked in Boaz's field during both the barley and wheat harvest (through June). By the end of the season, Naomi decided it was time for Ruth to find another husband and outlined a bold plan of action. She told Ruth to take a bath, put on perfume and her nicest dress, go down to the threshing floor and lay at Boaz's feet. Naomi assured Ruth that Boaz would tell her what to do (Ruth 3:1-4).

Ruth was obedient to Naomi's plan. Ruth lay at Boaz's feet, he woke up in the middle of the night, asked her what she was doing and she asked him to fulfill his role as kinsman-redeemer (Ruth 3:8-9) and Boaz agreed:

> *Although it is true that I am near of kin, there is a kinsman-redeemer nearer than I. Stay here for the night, and in the morning if he wants to redeem, good; let him redeem," he told her. "But if he is not willing, as surely as the Lord lives I will do it. Lie here until morning"* (Ruth 3:12-13).

Boaz recognized that Ruth had choices and commended her for choosing him:

> *The Lord bless you, my daughter!" Boaz exclaimed. "You are showing more family loyalty now than ever by not running after a younger man, whether rich or poor* (Ruth 3:10).

On the other hand, Boaz could have had his choice of women if for no other reason than that he had money, position, prestige and power. The Bible makes no reference to a previous marriage, concubines, his age or his appearance, but it does refer to his position in the community: *"Now there was a wealthy and influential man in Bethlehem named Boaz"* (Ruth 2:1).

Boaz was a man of his word. He told Ruth he would speak to the nearer kinsman redeemer and he did:

> *So Boaz went to the town gate and took a seat there. When the family redeemer he had mentioned came by, Boaz called out to him, "Come over here, friend. I want to talk to you." So they sat down together* (Ruth 4:1).

Boaz was probably disappointed when the nearer kinsman said he would redeem the property, and ecstatic when he declined the package deal of the property and Ruth:

You know Naomi who came back from Moab. She is selling the land that belonged to our relative Elimelech. I felt that I should speak to you about it so that you can redeem it if you wish. If you want the land, then buy it here in the presence of these witnesses. But if you don't want it, let me know right away, because I am next in line to redeem it after you." The man replied, "All right, I'll redeem it." Then Boaz told him, "Of course, your purchase of the land from Naomi also requires that you marry Ruth, the Moabite widow. That way, she can have children who will carry on her husband's name and keep the land in the family." "Then I can't redeem it," the family redeemer replied, "because this might endanger my own estate. You redeem the land; I cannot do it (Ruth 4:2-6, NLT).

Boaz was willing to put all he had—time, talent and treasure—on the line for Ruth, and the elders blessed the union:

May the Lord make the woman who is now coming into your home like Rachel and Leah, from whom all the nations of Israel descended! May you be great in Ephrathah and famous in Bethlehem. And may the Lord give you descendants by this young woman who will be like those of our ancestor Perez.... (Ruth 4:11-12)

It is interesting to note that when Boaz first met Ruth he spoke a blessing over her: *"May the Lord, the God of Israel, under whose wings you have come to take refuge, reward you fully"* (Ruth 2:12). He probably had no idea that one of the ways God would reward Ruth was through him. Boaz came to realize that although people need God to bless them, sometimes God uses people to implement the specific blessings He has in mind for His children.

Ruth and Boaz married and had a son named Obed, who had a son named Jesse, who had a son named David, all in the lineage of Jesus Christ. God orchestrated the meeting between Ruth and Boaz, the mutual attraction and the subsequent marriage. Ruth set herself up for God's blessings when she accepted Naomi's God: *"Your people will be my people, and your God will be my God"* (Ruth 1:16). By possessing their own vessels in sanctification and honor, Boaz and Ruth pleased God and were rewarded with the gifts of marriage and children.

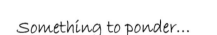

Something to ponder...

Have you ever been pleasantly surprised to meet someone you have heard about and discover that they live up to everything you heard about them? This was the way the first meeting between Boaz and Ruth went. Ruth may not have heard of Boaz, but he had certainly heard of her, and he was thrilled that her reputation hadn't been exaggerated. This is the question to ponder: What reputation precedes you?

When I graduated from high school, the goal of most of the girls in my class was to get married and have children. Some of them did exactly that and within a ten-year period were divorced and/or working on marriage number two or three. Sadly, very few are still married to their original spouses. Marriage wasn't anything I wanted to try because of the marriages I observed growing up, including my parents. I was raised in a two-parent household, but I never saw anything that would inspire me to want marriage, although I am sure my parents had what would have been considered a "good" marriage. I realized early on that I didn't want good; I wanted great.

It wasn't until I accepted Jesus Christ as Lord and Savior that I had a desire to get married. When I started attending First Church of God, I actually saw God's idea for marriage. Once I was at a point where I wanted to share my life with someone, I asked God about marriage and He said yes so I would periodically note the qualities I wanted in a husband. A lot of women have done the same, and there is nothing wrong with that as long as we don't become obsessed with the list and miss the real thing! If this is something you do, let me ask you a question: Once you get past the big three—Saved, Sanctified and filled with the Holy Ghost—do you know what you want?

WHAT DO YOU WANT ME TO DO FOR YOU?

God honors the desires of our hearts when our will is lined up with His. Keep in mind that God is not obligated to honor our suggestions. It is not enough to say, "I want a husband." We need to be more specific. The story of blind Bartimaeus is a perfect example of knowing what you want:

> Then they came to Jericho. As Jesus and His disciples, together with a large crowd, were leaving the city, a blind man, Bartimaeus (that is, the Son of Timaeus), was sitting by the roadside begging. When he heard that it was Jesus of Nazareth, he began to shout, "Jesus, Son of David, have mercy on me!" Many rebuked him and told him to be quiet, but he shouted all the more, "Son of David, have mercy on me!" Jesus stopped and said, "Call him." So they called to the blind man, "Cheer up! On your feet! He's calling you." Throwing his cloak aside, he jumped to his feet and came to Jesus. "What do you want me to do for you?" Jesus asked him. The blind man said, "Rabbi, I want to see." "Go," said Jesus, "your faith has healed you." **Immediately** he received his sight and followed Jesus along the road (Mark 10:46-52, emphasis mine).

This Bible passage gives us three clear examples to follow:

BE PERSISTENT

Bartimaeus was persistent in asking for a response. Matter of fact, some people would probably call his behavior obnoxious in that he didn't care who didn't like what he was doing. He was the blind man who made his living sitting by the road begging, not them.

What about you? Have you asked God for marriage and received a response? Or did you assume, for whatever reason, that God would not give you a husband so you haven't asked? How persistent are you when it comes to seeking God's will?

CHANGE YOUR ATTITUDE

Once the others told him that Jesus was asking for him, Bartimaeus changed his attire. He threw off the cloak that identified him as a blind person in anticipation of what was to come.

What about you? If you are single and believe that God has marriage for you, what do you need to throw off? What behavioral changes need to be made? If you are serious about getting married, then act like it.

ASK GOD FOR THE IMPOSSIBLE

Bartimaeus had heard enough about Jesus to believe that if he could just catch His attention, he would have a chance for his miracle. You see, Bartimaeus didn't need a blessing, he needed a miracle, and although physically blind he was able to recognize Jesus as the Miracle Worker. He had probably said to himself, "I've heard about what He has done throughout the region, and if I ever get a chance, I'm going to go for the gusto. Yeah, it would be nice to have a house and a job, but I want to see. I'm tired of having to be led only where other people are willing to take me. I'm tired of sitting on the ground begging. I want to see where I'm going. So I'm going to just step out in faith and ask for my sight, and the way I figure He only has two answers, yes or no. I believe He'll say yes, but I won't know unless I ask Him." When he caught Jesus' attention and Jesus asked him, *"What do you want me to do for you?"* Bartimaeus didn't say, "Oh, Lord, just bless me anyway you want." He was very specific, "Rabbi, I want to see." Bartimaeus didn't want a blessing; he wanted a miracle. And that is what he received.

What about you? Although God already knows everything, we need to be specific with our requests. Do you want a blessing or a miracle? A husband is a blessing; Boaz is a miracle. God already knows what you need better than you do, so the specifications are for you to be able to recognize Boaz when he comes.

DON'T JUST FOCUS ON THE SUPERFICIAL

Having the right address or job, dressing straight out of the fashion magazines, driving the latest status vehicle or being handsome is a poor substitute for God's best.

When thinking of your mates' attributes, please be sure to focus on integrity and character and not just looks and money. My son is the epitome of tall, dark and handsome. He was a pretty baby, a cute little boy and grew into a handsome man. While he was growing up, I cautioned him not to get caught up with girls who only focused on his looks. After spending time with him if all they could say is "he's fine," then they missed his substance. He is intelligent, funny, trustworthy, sensitive, caring, compassionate and on and on. Of course I'm biased, but my point is that when it comes to asking God for a mate, don't just focus on looks.

No one wants a person who is unattractive, but we shouldn't get so hung up on skin color, hair texture, facial features or height that we miss the bigger picture. Looks are important, but substance is greater. Looks fade (and if you don't believe me, just go to a high school, college or family reunion) and if that is the foundation of the relationship, you will be in trouble. Aging, sickness, overeating, physical neglect or stress can change the way one looks. There has to be something more. The more is what I call substance: The essence, integrity and character of a man. Substance is what will make or break the marriage even if the material assets are in place. Don't believe me? Just ask a woman who has the right address or drives the latest status vehicle but can't trust her husband.

Another component of substance is consistency. Remember Dr. Jekyll and Mr. Hyde? One was mild-mannered and the other was crazy, yet they were the same person. The last thing you need or should want is a man who appears one way and then changes without notice. It breaks my heart to see women connect with men who are saying the right thing to get them to the altar. Once the woman has invested her emotions, Mr. Hyde shows up a few months (or weeks!) after the wedding.

There is something you can do to make sure this doesn't happen to you: Don't jump into a relationship without having enough information to make an intelligent decision. Take time to discover the "real" man behind the image. Everyone is on his or her best behavior in the beginning, including you. All of us have a dark side and if we didn't stay under the Blood, our dark side would raise its ugly head on a regular basis. It takes time for the real person to come forth, and it happens by being in a variety of situations with your Boaz. How does he handle pressure? How does he handle being around children? What does he say about his co-workers or former girlfriends? How is his temper? How does he relate to your family? How does he relate to his family? Does he have road rage? How does he interact with other people? How does he act in public?

My caution is to make sure you take a long look before you leap. I'm not saying that you need to suspect every word or act, but I am saying that you need to take off the rose colored glasses and pay attention. The last thing you want is to go from the frying pan into the fire!

BE SURE TO INCLUDE THE NON-NEGOTIABLES

The non-negotiables are those things that you definitely will not consider in a mate. It is not fair to enter into any relationship with the intent of changing your man. You don't want him changing you, do you? It is okay to include the non-negotiables on your wish list, and don't let anyone tell you otherwise, because you are the person who will have to live with it, not your friends. Don't be afraid to ask yourself the hard question: Can I accept this forever?

One of the primary non-negotiables on my list is a man who smokes or uses any type of tobacco products. There are a lot of Christians who are still struggling with this habit, but I am not willing to wait for my man's deliverance in this area. I smoked for about twenty-one years (and you know what they say about reformed smokers) so I know it is a habit, but I also know the Habit Breaker! Smoking causes bad breath, the smell stays in your clothes, in your hair and on furniture. Smoking dulls your sense of smell and taste. Physically, smoking increases your risk of heart attacks and cancers of the lungs, mouth, throat, bladder, colon, rectum, pancreas and cervix. I have had three close relatives, including my father, die from lung cancer. My father's cancer was directly related to second-hand smoke. With that type of history does it make sense that I would contemplate a relationship with a man who smoked? I think not. And I caution you not to be so quick to accept bad habits from those around you. I know of couples who made temporary changes just to appease their mate only to relapse into former habits once the marriage takes place. While it is true that you cannot change someone else, it is also true that you can ask God to give you a better sense of discernment and then pay attention to what He shows you.

Another non-negotiable for me is a man who is ill-mannered. I grew up in an era where men were courteous to every woman they met, not just the good-looking ones. Consequently, I don't expect to open my own doors or struggle into a coat if a man is standing there. I don't get upset when a man displays manners. Can I open a door myself? Sure. But why should I not allow a man to show his respect by doing it for me? Now, I must confess I haven't always had this attitude, and I will give you two examples to prove my point.

In the early 1980s I went to Dallas, Texas and spent my first week in a luxury hotel. I had never had any man open a door for me until I arrived at this four-star hotel, but I got used to it real quick! When I arrived back home, the man I was seeing came to the airport to pick me up and when we got to his car, I stood beside the door waiting for him to open it, but he had gone around to his side, gotten in and rolled down the window wondering why I was still standing there! Obviously, I was back in the real world.

The other example happened several years ago. One of my co-workers and I had to go to a work site and he was going to drive. When we got to his car, I opened my own door and got in. When we got to the site, I opened my own door and got out. When we were ready to get back into the car he said, "Don't open that door!" and when I looked at him, he explained that he preferred to open the door for me. I laughed and told him I didn't have a problem with him doing that, but sometimes if you didn't open your own door, you would be left standing around.

Once you have created your non-negotiables, ask the Lord if you are being too picky. Your friends can only give you their opinions, which may or may not be a good thing, but God will lead you in the right direction. He knows what is ahead and what type of husband you need to achieve what He has planned for your life. We can be specific with our requests, but we must also be open to God changing our desires. You need a supporter, not a saboteur. You need a mate who is going to cheer you on to accomplish God's will for your life. What you don't need is someone who will sabotage your efforts. That is why you must allow God to choose your mate for you.

I have specifics on my wish list that the Lord may or may not honor. And I will admit that every now and then I contemplate compromising. Yet each time I am tempted, God sends a Word of reminder that His promise is still good and I can have what I want. (I believe the Word, and I will let you know how things turn out when I write the sequel to this book, *"I Waited for Boaz"*).

Something to ponder...

All of us have physical preferences and what you think looks good may only look good to you. One of my favorite movies is an old black and white called The Enchanted Cottage. The premise of the movie is that when you look at people you love, you don't see them the way others do. The female lead was plain and the male lead was once handsome, but became disfigured in a war. However, once they fell in love they were convinced that God had given them a miracle, because when they looked at each other they didn't see plain or disfigured. She was beautiful and he was once again handsome. To everyone else, though, they still looked exactly the same, because beauty is in the eye of the beholder. This is the question to ponder: How do you define beauty?

WHY WAIT FOR BOAZ?

Why should you wait for Boaz? Because he represents God's best. No one can love you like God, but we can experience God's love in human form if we wait for His gift to us. When I see women making wrong choices for mates, it breaks my heart. They are so excited going into the marriage only to be disappointed later in divorce court. God doesn't want that for His children, and neither do I.

Why not wait for the best God has? God is not going to give us all the same man, yet there are some basic characteristics that every Boaz will have.

Throughout the rest of this book you will discover that the biblical Boaz is a man of character and integrity; he is trustworthy, compassionate and caring, which are all good traits. He is also an astute businessman and an excellent negotiator. Your Boaz should possess those same qualities along with what I call the Five Ss: Spiritual, Secure, Stable, Sensitive and Sexy.

A *spiritual man* is one who understands that all of his help comes from the Lord. He knows he will never be the man, husband or father he was intended to be without God in his life. He knows he was created to praise God. He is sold out to God, not just going through the motions because it is the politically correct thing to do. He is a mighty man of God unashamedly in love with God. Because of that love, he is able to love you the way you deserve. He understands that submission is a two-way street and he has read and embraced all of Ephesians 5:22-33 (NLT):

> *For wives, this means submit to your husbands as to the Lord. For a husband is the head of his wife as Christ is the head of the church. He is the Savior of his body, the church. As the church submits to Christ, so you wives should submit to your husbands in everything. For husbands, this means love your wives, just as Christ loved the church. He gave up his life for her to make her holy and clean, washed by the cleansing of God's word. He did this to present her to himself as a glorious church without a spot or wrinkle or any other blemish. Instead, she will be holy and without fault. In the same way, hus-*

bands ought to love their wives as they love their own bodies. For a man who loves his wife actually shows love for himself. No one hates his own body but feeds and cares for it, just as Christ cares for the church. And we are members of his body. As the Scriptures say, "A man leaves his father and mother and is joined to his wife, and the two are united into one." This is a great mystery, but it is an illustration of the way Christ and the church are one. So again I say, each man must love his wife as he loves himself, and the wife must respect her husband.

A *secure man* knows who he is, whose he is and what he is about. He is not intimidated by what you bring to the relationship. He will encourage you to be your best. He is self-confident, self-assured and can handle however God blesses you. He understands that he is not in competition with you, but that you complement each other. When one of you succeeds you both succeed.

A *stable man* may not go to the gym twice a week, but he watches his diet, exercises and takes care of his health, so he is physically stable (or he is in the process of becoming so). He has put his past in perspective, which makes him emotionally stable (or he is in the process of becoming so). He is financially stable, regardless of his income, because he understands and embraces the concepts of tithing, offering, sowing and reaping.

A *sensitive man* understands that there are times when all his woman needs is the assurance that everything is going to be all right. He understands the difference between listening and fixing. He is a keeper! A close cousin to sensitivity is compassion and together they create a powerful duo.

A man is *sexy* when he knows that true sexiness has very little to do with the way he looks physically and everything to do with how he presents himself through behavior and speech.

So why am I willing to wait for Boaz? Because God expects me to accept the best He has to offer. If you have ever had an imitation anything and then experienced the real thing, it is as different as night and day. When I gave up caffeine, the thought of drinking anything other than the original cola I enjoyed was not acceptable. Why? Because I believed it was the best tasting and I would rather do without than accept a substitute. I apply that same principle to marriage. I would rather stay single than to accept a substitute for God's best. I don't want a good marriage, I want a great one, and that is what you get with Boaz for a husband.

The woman who waits for Boaz is committed to God and His plan for her life. She is in tune to who she is and what her purpose is. She has done the hard work of self-reflection (or is in the process) and realizes that she is already complete in Jesus Christ, her Lord and Savior. She has put her past in perspective and moved on. She knows how to take care of business, but isn't afraid of asking for help. She has it going on because she understands that all of her help comes from the Lord. This woman is not going to settle for anything less than God's best.

Questions for Reflection

1. Are you willing to wait for Boaz?
2. If you have started a wish list, what are the most important items on it?
3. What non-negotiables have you included on your list?
4. Can you think of any other qualities to add to the Five Ss?

Recommended Reading

Lady in Waiting by Debby Jones and Jackie Kendall
Settling for Less than God's Best: A Relationship Checkup for Single Women by Elsa Kok

Chapter Two
Don't Settle for B.O.Z.O.
The Power of Choice

Something happened a few years ago. I am not sure how or why or even exactly when. I observed some women beginning to believe one of the enemy's lies that they were not worth much. Or worse, that their value was directly related to having a man. The lie began insidiously creeping into every aspect of our society and eventually reached the church (ever had one of the church mothers ask when you were going to settle down?) The lie is reinforced every time a woman settles for B.O.Z.O. instead of waiting for B.O.A.Z. With the help of the Lord, that lie can stop today for those willing to accept this truth.

B.O.Z.O. is symbolic of those men who have yet to allow the Lord to take control of their life; B.O.A.Z. is symbolic of a man after God's own heart. An acronym for B.O.Z.O. could be **B**uilding **O**n **Z**eal **O**nly (trying to do things based only on their own strength) whereas an acronym for B.O.A.Z. could be **B**uilding **O**n the **A**lmighty's **Z**eal (allowing the Lord to have total control).

Please don't assume this chapter is an attempt at male bashing because it isn't. I love men and believe they are one of God's greatest creations right up there with the bluest sky and the greenest grass. But, just like a storm-colored sky is still sky and brown grass is still grass, a man not living up to his full potential is still a man, just not the best representation of the male species. There are men (and women) who are not worthy of our time, energy or effort. They are not about anything, and if we hang around too many of them too long we won't be about anything either!

My purpose for writing this chapter is to birth deep in your spirit a reluctance to settle for anything other than God's best in all areas of your life, especially marriage. Most of this chapter is the result of a conversation I had with three Christian men who confessed they were once a B.O.Z.O. and made the transition to B.O.A.Z.

How do you know if you have settled instead of waited? The following is based on personal observations; you may have your own qualifiers.

B.O.Z.O. OR B.O.A.Z.?

B.O.Z.O. is stuck in the past and cannot or will not move on. Have you ever met a man who lives in yesterday? His best time was middle school and he is now thirty-five? His best job was the one right out of high school and he is now sixty? His first girlfriend was the best, yet he has been with you for two years? You know the type. B.O.Z.O. stays stuck and sees no reason to get out of his rut (if he even realizes he is in one) and will have problems with you if you try to grow past him.

B.O.A.Z. has done the hard work of putting his past in perspective by dealing with the good, the bad and the ugly. He understands that his past contributes to his present and he has kept the good, put the bad behind him, turned the ugly over to the Lord and moved on.

B.O.Z.O. is always getting ready, but nothing ever gets accomplished. Again, you might know a man like this. "One day" is his favorite opening line and "coulda," "woulda," "shoulda" are permanent parts of his vocabulary. I am talking about the get-rich-quick dreamer who will waste his time (and yours if you let him) always getting ready but never accomplishing anything.

B.O.A.Z. has a plan, steps out in faith and puts the plan into action. If the first one doesn't work, he will try something else. He will never throw up his hands, say "Oh, well!" and then stop trying.

B.O.Z.O. will not work or cannot keep a job. Cut your losses now. This man will never be able to support you financially because he will never have the means. I am convinced there is something wrong with a woman who becomes involved with a man who stays home while she goes off to work day after day after day because he won't work. Of course, there are extenuating circumstances—layoffs, sickness, et cetera. I am not talking about those types of situations. I am talking about a BUM, a man who refuses to get or keep a job. There is always going to be something wrong with any job he takes because the problem is not everybody else, it is him. It is always somebody else's fault and B.O.Z.O. usually says, "If *they* would do this, then *I* would do that."

B.O.A.Z. owns the company, and if he doesn't it is only because God hasn't released him yet. While employed for someone else, B.O.A.Z. is a productive part of the team. He is developing and enhancing his skills so that when God does release him, he is ready to go.

B.O.Z.O. cannot keep you in the style to which you are accustomed, regardless of what that style is. Do you know women who used to have their hair and nails done on a regular basis or dressed nice but couldn't continue the practice once they got involved with certain men? Again, there may be extenuating circumstances, but perhaps B.O.Z.O. is draining them financially and they can't afford to take care of themselves because they are too busy taking care of him.

B.O.A.Z. lives within his means. He is frugal, but not stingy. He has sound financial plans and goals. He may not be able to give you everything, but at least he won't ask to borrow money to pay for the stuff he buys you!

B.O.Z.O. encourages you to lower your standards. Any man who encourages you to change your morals or scruples in a negative way is not for you (no matter how innocent or subtle his suggestions appear). People are invited into your life to enhance it, not diminish it. When you connect with a man who drastically causes a negative change in your routine, you are headed in a dangerous direction.

B.O.A.Z. will remind you of God's standard and will never put you in a compromising position. That is not to say he has a halo on his head, but it is to say that he loves the Lord too much to intentionally bring dishonor to God, himself or you.

B.O.Z.O. treats other women better than you. This is the man who will jump to open the door for another woman and let it slam in your face. He puts on a show of affection only when others are around, but treats you like a dog when it is just the two of you. It is disrespectful and disgusting.

B.O.A.Z. treats you like a queen. It has been said that if you want to know how a man will treat you, look at how he treats his mother. B.O.A.Z. treats his mother (and all the other women in his life) just fine.

MAKING THE TRANSITION FROM B.O.Z.O. TO B.O.A.Z.

Allow me to remind you that B.O.Z.O. is not always a sinner. There are a number of men who have accepted Jesus Christ as their Lord and Savior who are now in a transitional stage. They recognize that their old behavior is no longer acceptable. The challenge then becomes one of B.O.Z.O. waiting for the change to B.O.A.Z. to occur. Some of the ways he will know the transition is complete will be:

- When he no longer places his needs above others.
- When he becomes a productive part of his church and community.

- When he takes his rightful position as the head of his home.
- When he releases the issues from his past.
- When he recognizes that outside of Christ he can do nothing.
- When he realizes that even when he can't see the progress, God is still working in his life.

The other challenge is for the sisters not to jump ahead of God and interfere in the transitional process. In most churches the ratio of women to men is two-to-one, if not higher, and unfortunately some women are more eager and aggressive than others. However, no one wants anything half done, and that is what you end up with if you attach yourself to B.O.Z.O. before he has made the transition to B.O.A.Z.

It is my understanding that some twelve-step programs encourage those in recovery to refrain from relationships during their first year. I wish the Church would adopt that practice. Some Christian women don't allow men enough time to get rooted and grounded in the Word and ways of God before they decide it is time for a relationship. When it doesn't turn out as expected, they want to point fingers at the man instead of taking responsibility for the part they played in the mess.

This all adds to the confusion and division among singles in the Church. A few rebels make other women look bad, and instead of making a distinction between those with good sense and those without, some men clump all women into the same category. When you come along being friendly, they act like you are ready to pick out china patterns and linen! Recognize this tactic as a trick of the devil. Think about it. If the devil can keep men and women at odds, how would families ever be established? If you can't even get the opposite sex to speak to each other, how would they interact, date, court or marry? I was the singles' coordinator at my church for almost seven years and one of my biggest challenges was getting men involved. When I asked why they weren't, their response usually included something about desperate women. I couldn't get upset at what they said because I know some (and you probably do, too). That is not to say there aren't desperate men in the church, because I know some of them, too.

My point is that a man making the transition from B.O.Z.O. to B.O.A.Z. has enough to worry about without having to deal with the intricacies of a new relationship. So, sisters, if you are one of the eager beavers who think that God needs help, I have a Word from the Lord for you: SNAP OUT OF IT!

SOMETHING TO PONDER

I once attended a women's class where the facilitator made the statement that a woman needed a man to make her complete (that word again!) and feel like a woman. I was offended, but I understood where she was coming from. This was an older sister whose generation taught women to marry for provision and protection. Some of these women were taught that they were somehow inferior if they didn't have a husband and/or children. Praise God for changing times! We have gained better understanding of what it means to be whole individuals, whether a man or woman, single or married. God has equipped us to take care of ourselves with His help. I strongly believe in marriage and the role of the man as the head of the house. However, I don't believe in waiting idly for Prince Charming to come along. I need to be about my Father's business and that includes taking care of me with His help. I will be more than happy to relinquish some control when B.O.A.Z. comes! What about you?

Questions for Reflection

1. If there is a B.O.Z.O. in your life, encourage him to persevere in staying before the Lord so the transition to B.O.A.Z. can be complete. Or perhaps he is not even at that point yet. Either way, pray for him and bless him with a copy of *Loose That Man and Let Him Go* by Bishop T. D. Jakes.
2. What other characteristics would you add for B.O.Z.O. and B.O.A.Z.?
3. Do you know what God wants for you in terms of a mate?
4. How much thought have you given to the changes marriage will bring to your life?

Recommended Reading

Knight in Shining Armor by P. B. Wilson
Making Peace with Your Past by H. Norman Wright

Chapter Three
Sister, Can We Talk?
The Power of Self-Examination

The B.O.Z.O. mentality is a mindset and a lifestyle that believes, in part, that someone owes you something. There are women—Bozettas—who believe that their physical attributes are all they need to get by. Bozetta very seldom makes an effort to get involved with life. Everything revolves around her and her needs and desires. If women should be running from B.O.Z.O., men should also avoid Bozetta like the plague.

WHOSE REPORT WILL YOU BELIEVE?

I believe women who settle for B.O.Z.O. do so because some have bought into the lie that says they are not attractive enough, smart enough, small enough, big enough, tall enough, short enough, fat enough, skinny enough—whatever—and if they don't grab hold of the first man who shows an interest, they will be left alone forever. But remember the children of Israel? In their rebellion they rejected God's best (Himself) and settled for God's good (Saul). Even after Saul was removed and David became King, he was still no more than God's better. Why? Because God's best is always going to be God's choice, and His choice is never going to be B.O.Z.O.!

Some women have a tendency to believe they have to settle because they are unclear of who they are. Once we recognize and accept our rightful position in God we grow up and stop doing certain things. We begin to focus on God and His desires for our lives. More importantly, we begin to believe what God says about us. The Bible is full of God's love for us, and I am sure you have favorite Bible passages. Just in case you don't, allow me to paraphrase some of mine. God says:

- I love you so much, I made you in my image (Genesis 1:27)
- I love you so much, I have tattooed your name on the palm of my hand (Isaiah 49:21)
- I love you so much, every hair on your head is numbered (Matthew 10:30)
- I love you so much, I made big plans for you before you were born (Jeremiah 1:5)
- I love you so much, I have made you the head and not the tail (Deuteronomy 28:13)
- I love you so much, I will finish whatever I start (Philippians 1:6)
- I love you so much, I have created a way of escape from temptation (1 Corinthians 10:13)
- I love you so much, I allowed My child to die for you (John 3:16)

So, whose report will you believe? The world's report says there is a shortage of men so you better grab the first person who smiles and shows you attention. Or, if you are tired of waiting on a man, you can always turn to a woman. But, praise God, the Lord's report says:

> *Your heavenly Father already knows all your needs and He will give you all you need from day to day if you live for Him and make the Kingdom of God your primary concern* (Matthew 6:33, NLT).

TURN ON THE LIGHT

God gives us the ability to choose for a purpose. However, our responsibility is to ensure that we don't allow negative factors to influence the choices we make. Some of those negative factors include low self-esteem, emotional issues or trauma or drama from our past. No one wants to be around a person with a lot of baggage. We must allow the Lord to expose the painful areas and help us deal with them so we can move on. Aren't you tired of going around in circles? Don't you want to know why you consistently make the same poor choices? Aren't you curious as to why you gravitate to or attract a certain type of man? Healing begins when we learn to confront our past. If we don't feel good about ourselves, chances are the people around us don't necessarily feel good about us either.

In the 1980s a well-known pop singer made a video showing him walking down the street. As his foot touched a segment of the sidewalk it would light up. Once his foot touched a different segment of the sidewalk, the previously lit one went dark. There is a lot of theological truth in that portion of the video because God only shines the spotlight on an area He wants us to concentrate on. Once we have obeyed, He spotlights another area and darkens the one we just left. We are not to worry about what is behind us because that is finished: *"But forget all that—it is nothing compared to what I am going to do"* (Isaiah 43:18, NLT). We are only to concentrate on what is ahead.

Dealing with the painful issues of our life is a lot like the video. But you know what? God only spotlights an area He knows we are ready to deal with, regardless of how painful we think it is. If we are not willing to be obedient, we can never be all God wants us to be. And we have no right to ask God for something if we are not doing what He has already said either via His Word, the pulpit or mature saints.

If you believe God has marriage as part of His plan for your life, then you should be waiting for B.O.A.Z. However, this is not the time to be idle. You should be using this time for God to deal with the issues in your life. If you have ever thought, "When I get married, I am going to ___" now is the time to be doing whatever that is. Of course, there are some pleasures only reserved for marriage, but if you have thought about buying a house, buy it; if you have thought about going back to school, go; if you have thought about children, adopt or foster. Marriage is not the be-all and end-all. If there are things you desire, and God agrees, go for it. After all, B.O.A.Z. is usually not attracted to a woman with a lot of excess baggage or frustrated dreams. This is the time to put your dreams into motion.

Something to ponder...

The attributes of the virtuous woman in Proverbs 31:10-30 are what Christian women should be striving for. This woman is gentle and kind, organized, possesses an entrepreneurial spirit, offers wise council, is well thought of by her children and is so connected to God that she possesses the heart of her husband because he trusts her. Question: How close are you to achieving Proverbs 31 status?

THE COURTING CHALLENGE

Sometimes people use the word "dating" to encompass everything prior to marriage. For the sake of clarification allow me to share my interpretation of the difference between dating and courting. "Dating" is going out with the opposite sex with the intent of fun and companionship and can be used as a tool to determine if a relationship needs to go to the next level. Anytime two or more people have agreed to do a specific thing at a specific time that is a date. It is not exclusive and can easily be done in a group.

"Courting" according to the *American Heritage Dictionary (2nd College Edition),* is "seeking affection with the intent to marry," which is very different from dating. That is not to say that once a relationship moves from dating to courting you will get married. You may discover something during the courting stage that causes you to realize that marrying this person is not God's will for you. However, it is during the courting stage that you will get into more involved dialogue about dreams and desires and will begin to discuss the important aspects of marriage—children, housing, where to spend holidays, finances, previous sexual history and so on. It is too early to have these conversations during the dating stage; yet, talking about certain subjects too early is a mistake that quite a few women (and men) make in an effort to create a sense of intimacy.

The Latin word for intimate (where the word intimacy comes from) means "innermost." In order to prevent living with regret after a relationship ends, my caution would be to guard against becoming too intimate too quickly, or sharing your innermost with someone before either of you are ready. Usually the regret comes from having shared something that you wish you could take back such as a physical or intellectual intimacy. Ecclesiastes 3:1 reminds us, *"There is a time for everything, and a season for every activity under heaven,"* including intimacy.

Although I am not a professional counselor, I have literally talked with hundreds of people, both married and single, about relationships. One of the things I have discovered is that more than half of the problems in marriage begins with choosing the wrong person to court. Although for some women the handwriting is on the wall, there is denial about what is really going on. Although God has convicted you, your friends have cautioned you and even your enemies have questioned why the two of you are together, you refuse to see what is right in front of your face. You try to explain it away by saying that you prayed about it. Perhaps you did, but did you wait for an answer from God? A lot of times we are too impatient to wait for God's response. If He doesn't respond right away (and especially if it is something we want to do anyway), we will convince ourselves that it's okay. Anytime the phrases "I know he will change..." "He didn't mean to do it..." or "I know it's not right, but..." becomes part of your vocabulary, you are headed for trouble.

Courting is challenging unless you understand that one of the primary purposes of this stage is to gather enough information to make a sound, biblical decision for marriage. I don't endorse the school of thought taught in some churches that Christians shouldn't date or court before marrying because that doesn't make sense. How else would you find out pertinent information? By the same token, I don't believe you need to stay in the courting period for years before you realize the relationship isn't working. That doesn't mean the involved parties aren't nice people; it just means they are not appropriate for each other, and they need to be released to find their true mate.

In the previous chapter we looked at B.O.Z.O. and B.O.A.Z. Perhaps after doing the comparison you realized you are courting B.O.Z.O. and he is not willing to make the transition to B.O.A.Z., but you are staying in the relationship because you don't want to be alone. If you are in a relationship only for convenience, that is inappropriate. A child of God never has an excuse for staying in an inappropriate relationship. My sister, if you are involved with B.O.Z.O., get out of the relationship now. Chances are real good that things are not going to get better. You don't have the ability to change anyone other than yourself, and you can't change yourself without God's help. Staying in an unhealthy relationship may mean you are blocking one of God's blessings for you: Your true soul mate. I know that change is never easy and sometimes we develop an unhealthy dependence on others and become reluctant to rock the boat. But don't you want God's best? If you are serious about marriage, then you should be serious about courting. Spending time with B.O.Z.O. is not productive.

In the 1970s there was an R&B group called The Whispers who had a song with a line that said, "I just meant to wet my feet, but you pulled me in where the waters of love run deep." The song was about one person playing a game and discovering too late that he or she had been caught in their own trap. It happened because they let their guard down and got comfortable. They may have even said, "I know he's not "the one," but it will give me something to do." Listen to me, FIND SOMETHING ELSE TO DO!

It is not enough to ask the Lord to help you if you don't really want to be helped. *"Above all else, guard your heart for it is the wellspring of life"* (Proverbs 4:23). To prevent disappointment, heartache and hurt, ask the Lord to guard your heart and emotions. You cannot play with fire without getting burned, and that is what happens when you don't guard your emotions. You will end up in a relationship that God never intended for you. God must be in control, and you must be willing to submit to His will, even if you don't like it!

If you are involved in an inappropriate relationship, I believe there are three initial corrective steps you must take:

REPENT

You may need to ask the Lord to forgive you for not trusting Him with your life and for not believing that He knew what and whom you needed. This is not the time to be cute; you need to come clean with God and get your life back on track. God is in no way obligated to correct your wrongs if you are not willing to repent for them.

You may also need to repent for having premarital sex (including intercourse, oral sex, masturbation [mutual or solitary], telephone sex, inappropriate chat room dialogues,

41

playing the "touchy-feely" game, sexting or any and all of the other creative ways the saints have devised to circumvent what the Word says about premarital sex). You do remember that sexual immorality is still a sin, right?

- *The body is not meant for sexual immorality, but for the Lord, and the Lord for the body* (1 Corinthians 6:13b).

- *Flee from sexual immorality. All other sins a man commits are outside his body, but he who sins sexually sins against his own body. Do you not know that your body is a temple of the Holy Spirit, who is in you, whom you have received from God? You are not your own; you were bought at a price. Therefore honor God with your body* (1 Corinthians 6:18-20).

- *But among you there must not be even a hint of sexual immorality, or of any kind of impurity, or of greed, because these are improper for God's holy people* (Ephesians 5:3).

- *It is God's will that you should be sanctified: that you should avoid sexual immorality; that each of you should learn to control his own body in a way that is holy and honorable, not in passionate lust like the heathen, who do not know God...* (1 Thessalonians 4:3-5).

As you can see, these verses don't allow any wiggle room for self-interpretation and destroys the argument of personal conviction: "God hasn't convicted me, so it must be okay." Sexual purity isn't about individual preference; it is about what God says, and He does not contradict His Word.

You are the only one who knows exactly what, when and why you need to repent. If you are unclear, ask God to show you. Trust me, He will!

GET TO A PLACE WHERE YOU CAN CLEARLY HEAR FROM GOD

You do this by getting quiet before the Lord, being open to His leading and being willing to do whatever He says. Getting quiet involves turning off the television, cell phones, CD/MP3 players and any and everything else that is a distraction. It also includes fasting and praying. Get into God's Word so He can give you a Word. God uses a variety of ways to speak to us, but whatever He says will always be consistent with His Word.

STAND STILL

Some people believe that after they ask for forgiveness, they just pick back up where they left off. Wrong! You have already proven you don't know what you're doing, so stand still and let God tell you the next move. Whatever you do, don't move until God (not your friends) gives you clear direction.

After you have done the above steps, the Lord may lead you to seek additional help in the form of counseling or an accountability partner. If this is His direction, please don't allow fear or pride to hold you back. Remember, God always has our best interest in mind when He gives us direction: *"For I know the plans I have for you, says the Lord..."* (Jeremiah 29:11a).

In spite of B.O.Z.O. being companionship and filling an empty space, you were not made for him and he is not worthy of you. If you are courting B.O.Z.O., stop wasting your time. Take a deep breath, get a grip and move on! Jesus is waiting to give you strength for the journey if you will only trust Him. Open your hand to God. Doing so means that you lose what you have been clinging to, but it also means that an empty hand is a hand that God can fill with what He desires for you.

Obieray Rogers

Get Into You
(A poem by Carrie Hudson)

Get into you; find out what's true
Re-evaluate your thoughts and accept whatever loss comes
from moving on.
Get into love and examine your heart
Clear out the fake images and fight to wake up
What feels natural to you.
Fight for yourself and stop defending the curse
That has robbed you of your peace of mind.
Get free at all cost, and again accept the loss that comes
from moving on.
Move on. Move on. Move on. Move on. Move on.

Questions for Reflection

1. Is there any appropriate way to be intimate without
   marriage?
2. How well do you know yourself? Do you know what
   you can and can't handle?
3. Why is it so hard for you to let go and let God?
4. Do you really believe that God loves you?

Recommended Reading

Woman, Thou Are Loosed! by Bishop T. D. Jakes
Just Enough Light for the Step I'm On by Stormie Omartian
Do You Think I'm Beautiful? by Angela Thomas

Chapter Four
What's Love Got To Do With It?
The Power of Attraction

Attraction is powerful and dangerous if it is not handled appropriately because it has the ability to both bless and destroy. By that I mean if you are prone to gravitate toward a certain type of man who is not God's will for you, and if you allow the attraction to go unchecked, it can destroy you, your walk and your witness.

Ruth caught Boaz's attention because she was working in his field. He recognized she was an unfamiliar face and inquired from his foreman as to who she was. Once he identified her as Naomi's daughter-in-law, Boaz gave her special attention. I believe this was partly because of her faithfulness to Naomi and also because he was attracted to her physically. His courtesy went beyond appreciation of her taking care of his deceased relative's wife. I believe that if he just wanted to show appreciation, he could have stopped at protecting her virtue by having her working with his people and having them drop handfuls of grain on purpose for her. He went beyond courtesy when he allowed her to drink the water drawn by his servants, when he invited her to share lunch with his reapers and then when he served her himself, something that was usually not done by the owner of the field.

Boaz wanted Ruth to know he was attracted to her. He was subtle with his attention. He didn't overpower her, but he was astute enough to know that Naomi would pick up on what was going on when Ruth came home with an overflow of grain. You have to remember that she came home the first day with twenty-eight pounds of grain, which was much more than would have normally been accumulated. Naomi and Ruth were childless widows taking care of themselves. Boaz was smart in that he gave Ruth something she needed—food—instead of flowers. That is not to say that flowers aren't wonderful, but my point is that Boaz took the time to think of what the immediate need was and that was for food. Perhaps he wanted her to know that not only *could* he provide for her, but that he *would* provide for her. I can't think of too many things more pleasing than someone taking the time to think about what I would like instead of doing business as usual, i.e., flowers and candy. There is nothing wrong with flowers or candy, but a gift is so much better when a little thought has been used.

We don't know how much time elapsed between Mahlon's death and Ruth moving to Bethlehem. If Boaz had approached her from a romantic aspect, there is a very good possibility that he may have offended her and she would have shut down on him, even if she were considered a second-class citizen in that culture. Instead he approached her from a subtle and more practical standpoint. Instead of asking for her phone number, he had his servants leave handfuls of grain on purpose.

The fact that his workers took him at his word and left so much indicates they noticed there was something special about her that had caught the eye of their boss. Perhaps they felt it was time for him to get married and decided to help him out. Maybe he had been grumpier than usual, and they decided he needed a wife. Maybe that is why the foreman gave her such a glowing report. Boaz simply asked who she was, and the foreman not only told him who she was, but where she was from and how long and how hard she had been working in the field, which only goes to show that you never know who is watching you.

Boaz had an excellent working relationship with his people, so perhaps he was close to his foreman and had sat around talking on various occasions. Perhaps Boaz had mentioned something about the qualities he would like Mrs. Boaz to have, and when the foreman said all the good things about Ruth, something clicked for him. I like the foreman's attitude because although Ruth would have been closer in social status to the foreman than Boaz, that didn't stop him from singing her praises to Boaz.

One of the things I love about this story is that Ruth wasn't paying any attention to Boaz and wouldn't have approached him if Naomi hadn't instructed her. She wasn't looking for romance, but that is usually the way it happens: You are minding your own business and God's choice is standing in front of you. Someone like Naomi has to give you a nudge in the right direction for you to begin paying attention. The foreman gave her the set-up, and she didn't even know it. Ruth's name means "satisfied," and Ruth was satisfied with what she had. She had been satisfied in Moab. She had been satisfied with Mahlon. She had been satisfied traveling with Naomi to a foreign land. But God had more He wanted her to be satisfied with and He gave her an unexpected blessing. Bethlehem may have been her destination, but Boaz was her destiny.

Boaz knew he was related to Elimelech and knew that Naomi had returned with her daughter-in-law. He probably didn't give it much thought until he actually saw Ruth. Although her request for protection involved marriage, Boaz didn't have to marry her. He would have been within the Law to just make sure that she and Naomi were taken care of and could have honored his duty as kinsman redeemer as a protector and not as a protective husband. He chose to interpret Ruth's request as a request for marriage. He had already demonstrated his attraction to her and interpreted her request for protection as a sign of her attraction for him.

No one wants to put their feelings on the line, which is why I admire men when they ask you for a date. They have no way of knowing whether you are going to accept or reject their invitation. There is nothing worse than a one-sided attraction, and Boaz was smart enough to know that he had to wait for a sign from Ruth before he pursued her further. When she approached him on the threshing floor, he got what he wanted.

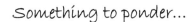

Something to ponder...

Just because a man isn't right for you doesn't mean you can't introduce him to your friends. After all, there had to have been some good quality that caught your attention, right? Of course, there is a right and wrong way to do this. If you are going to introduce a man who wasn't right for you to one of your friends, please remember to use what is sometimes called the "sandwich approach." Start with a positive, insert a negative and end with a positive. I had a woman spend fifteen minutes telling me all the things wrong with a man she had recently met and then said, "But he'd be perfect for you!" Obviously, she had never heard of this approach.

Questions for Reflection

1. How do you know when you are attracted to a man?
2. How do you handle a man's attraction?
3. How satisfied are you with where God has you?

Recommended Reading

The Five Love Languages by Gary Chapman
Single, Married, Separated and Life after Divorce by Myles Munroe

Chapter Five
If I Could Turn Back Time
The Power of Self-Control

Have you ever said to yourself, "If I could turn back time, I would …?" I know I have more times than I care to admit. Making decisions contrary to or outside of God's will can't help but result in regret.

I recently read an article about a pop singer who came on the music scene several years ago unashamedly believing in abstinence. In this article she was confessing that she had only slept with one man (another pop singer), because after two years of being together she believed he was "the one." She didn't realize that they would have a very public breakup shortly thereafter.

Many women fall into this same trap. Instead of waiting for the wedding night, they anticipate their wedding vows because they are convinced they have met "the one" and don't realize that a lot can happen before saying "I do." Someone has called it seeking to fulfill a legitimate need in an illegitimate way, which is true. Sexual urges and desires are God-given gifts. It is our assignment to wait until the proper time to open the gift. When you were younger, did you ever sneak a peak at a gift and then try to rewrap it? No matter how careful you were, there was usually some indication that things were not as they should be and you got caught. Premarital sex is like trying to rewrap a gift. No matter how hard you try, there are some things that once given away can never be recovered.

THE BENEFITS OF EXERCISING SELF-CONTROL

Ruth worked in Boaz's field from April to June. They were accustomed to seeing each other on a regular basis although there is no indication conversation took place each time. Yet, there was something about Ruth that appealed to Boaz on a male-female level. To go to bed alone and wake up to discover someone you are attracted to laying at your feet is very tempting.

I must confess that Naomi telling Ruth to lie at Boaz's feet has always puzzled me. I unsuccessfully researched numerous commentaries to determine what the significance of that particular instruction was and I finally ended up calling the Melton Center for Jewish Studies at The Ohio State University. I asked them if this was a custom of that time and was assured that it was not, but that it referred more to an act of humility. Ruth had already shown humility by being willing to glean for a living, and Naomi felt that her spirit was receptive to this next set of instructions. The bottom line is that Ruth trusted Naomi and believed in her wisdom and maturity, which says something about Naomi's character. However, this does not mean that Ruth was naïve. I believe if Boaz had not treated her as well as he had, or had not conducted himself in an appropriate manner during the time she had been gleaning, she would not have been receptive to going to the threshing floor.

The plan had the appearance of sneakiness to it; yet, in a way it was so simple that it actually made sense. Ruth and Boaz had worked around each other for approximately three months during both the wheat and barley harvest. Naomi knew that Boaz was a near kinsman (although as we know, there was one closer). Perhaps Naomi knew of the other kinsman but wanted Boaz for Ruth instead of the nearer relative. Perhaps she knew that the other kinsman would not be willing to put his reputation and inheritance in jeopardy by marrying Ruth and that Boaz would. Whatever the reason, Naomi told Ruth exactly what to do to move the relationship to the next level. (I certainly hope that no one takes this as encouragement to walk up to men asking them for marriage!). Naomi knew that there was an attraction between Ruth and Boaz and decided to help that attraction.

During my research I discovered several theories regarding what happened that night on the threshing floor. One commentator was convinced that Ruth and Boaz had sexual intercourse on the threshing floor. Another believed just the opposite and stated that Ruth went to the threshing floor pure and left pure. Still another pointed out that the law of the kinsman redeemer could not be fulfilled if the two parties had sexual intercourse prior to marriage. The laws regarding sexual purity were in place long before Ruth and Boaz were born, and I refuse to believe that God contradicts His Word, regardless of the circumstances.

Boaz's name means "in strength," and he used strength to exercise self-control on the threshing floor. Boaz does not come across as a hypocrite, and I can't imagine him protecting Ruth's reputation after spending the night having sexual relations. If he had treated her like a loose woman, he could have cared less whether anyone saw her leave the threshing floor. I believe he respected her enough to put his sexual feelings on hold to fulfill his destiny. Approximately twenty-eight generations later, one of Boaz's descendants would also put his sexual feelings on hold to fulfill his destiny:

> *This is how the birth of Jesus Christ came about: His mother Mary was pledged to be married to Joseph, but before they came together, she was found to be with child through the Holy Spirit. Because Joseph her husband was a righteous man and did not want to expose her to public disgrace, he had in mind to divorce her quietly. But after he had considered this, an angel of the Lord ap-*

peared to him in a dream and said, "Joseph son of David, do not be afraid to take Mary home as your wife, because what is conceived in her is from the Holy Spirit. She will give birth to a Son, and you are to give Him the name Jesus, because He will save His people from their sins." All this took place to fulfill what the Lord had said through the prophet: "The virgin will be with child and will give birth to a Son, and they will call Him Immanuel–which means, "God with us." When Joseph woke up, he did what the angel of the Lord had commanded him and took Mary home as his wife. **But he had no union with her until she gave birth to a Son.** *And he gave Him the name Jesus* (Matthew 1:18-25, emphasis mine).*

Ruth and Boaz could have engaged in sexual intercourse and then tried to cover it up. Ruth could have tried to trick him and pretend ignorance. After all, she was originally from Moab and a former idol worshipper. Ruth could have said, "Oops, I didn't know I wasn't supposed to do that," and fallen back on having been an idol worshipper longer than a believer in God. She could have said, "I thought Naomi told me to get in bed with you," instead of just laying at Boaz's feet. She could have used the "I need sex on a regular basis" excuse since she had been married for ten years. There are a number of excuses Ruth could have used, but praise God she didn't.

Boaz could have used her, and it would have been her word against his. When Boaz woke up and found Ruth at his feet, she took a chance on her reputation being destroyed. Boaz could have taken advantage of her by treating her like a loose woman. After all, "good girls" didn't hang out on the threshing floor in the middle of the night. He could have agreed to fulfill the role of kinsman redeemer after he sampled the goods "to make sure they fit." He could have claimed that he drank too much. Instead, he sought to protect her reputation once she identified herself and why she was there, and encouraged her to leave early in the morning: *"Don't let it be known that a woman came to the threshing floor"* (Ruth 3:14) and he gave her a parting gift: *"...Bring me the shawl you are wearing and hold it out. When she did so, he poured into it six measures of barley and put it on her"* (Ruth 3:15). The grain had a two-fold purpose: It was another gift to show his affection, but it would also be a sign to Naomi that Ruth's request was going to be granted. If Ruth had returned home empty-handed, Naomi may have rightly perceived that Boaz had rejected Ruth.

So what are the benefits of self-control? For Ruth it was a new name, new address, children and elevated social status. For Boaz it was a woman he could respect and trust. For both of them it was God's favor and lineage in the life of Jesus Christ.

For today's Christian it is assurance that we are pleasing God. I know of several couples who have dated, courted and married without having premarital sex. Was it easy? No. Were they tempted to give in? Absolutely! Was it worth it on the wedding night? Hallelujah! By being obedient to God's Word, He has blessed them abundantly, I believe, as a way of expressing His pleasure at them possessing their vessels with honor.

When you compare the benefits of self-control to a few minutes of premature pleasure, it puts everything else in context. *"And your Father, who knows all secrets, will reward you"* (Matthew 6:18, NLT).

THE CHALLENGE OF SELF-CONTROL

Having self-control is sometimes easier said than done because we don't like to deny ourselves what we perceive to be pleasurable activities.

My father was an alcoholic and after seeing and experiencing that particular devastation I very seldom drank. I have never liked being out of control, so I experimented very little with drugs. I smoked cigarettes for twenty-one years, quit shortly after being saved and never had the urge to start again. However, sex is another story all together because it was my preferred sin before salvation. I have been saved and celibate for a long time, and I am not about to tell you that I never have the urge for physical release or inappropriate intimacy. Please! I am not that deep! Yet, I can tell you that it is possible to live holy and maintain abstinence without losing your mind. God knew exactly what He was doing when He placed me in a holiness church where the Bible is clearly taught and preached. There is no way I can say I don't understand, so if I sin it will be by choice and not out of ignorance. Is it always easy to do the right thing? No. But with God's help, you can be victorious over every area of your life that you are willing to turn over to Him.

Physical urges can come upon you at any time, and you must have your own reasons for why you are willing to stay sexually pure in addition to what the Bible says. It would be nice if the Bible were enough, but some people like to pick and choose which Bible verses they will obey. For me there are several reasons I will not give in when the urge hits:

- I believe that having premarital sex would disappoint God. It is one thing not to like what someone does; it is a totally different thing to actually be disappointed in someone. I never want to do anything to disappoint God.

- God has entrusted me with ministering to His people, and I have a duty to walk worthy of my calling. Does that mean I never make mistakes? No. But it does mean that there are certain mistakes I am not going to make. I don't believe in starting things that aren't going to be finished, so I don't intentionally set myself up for sexual temptations.

- There are too many sexually transmitted diseases going around to take a chance (nineteen million new cases per year according to the 2010 Kinsey Institute report). The reality is that some men are unwilling or unable to tell the truth (for whatever reason), so even if I ask if they have been tested for AIDS or other STDs, I can't be sure of their answer. It is not worth it.

- There is a very real chance of poor performance. I have been around enough to know not to believe the media hype regarding sex. According to them, when you engage in sexual intercourse everything is perfect, fireworks occur and you have multiple orgasms all night long. That may happen every now and then, but it is unrealistic to believe it is going to happen every time. It takes time to get the rhythm right and discover the likes and dislikes of your partner, so unless I am planning on continuously sinning, the first time may be more awkward than awesome!

What has that self-control gotten me? Peace with God, peace of mind and a good reputation. When I minister to God's people, I am not worried about people looking around to see how many of my former lovers are sitting in the audience or calling me a hypocrite.

LET'S TALK ABOUT LUST

I once had a woman tell me that she didn't know how she ended up in bed with a man. When she first said it I thought to myself: How could you not know? Weren't you there? However, the more I thought about it, the more I realized that she was probably right, especially if she was under the control of lust. Lust is a powerful emotion.

One definition of lust is "an overwhelming desire or craving; an intense or unrestrained sexual craving." Lust should be considered one of the silent killers because when you are in the throes of it you are not as cautious as you should be. One of the reasons sexually transmitted diseases are still on the rise is because people don't want to stop to protect themselves—they are only interested in living for the moment. But that moment may kill you. That is why you can't play with lust and you need to know yourself. There are things you may be able to handle that someone else can't or vice versa. I have single Christian female friends who don't have a problem with watching R-rated movies or listening to songs with suggestive lyrics or even dating unsaved men. That is not my experience.

God knew we were going to be tempted, so He inspired Paul to write:

> *No temptation has seized you except what is common to man. And God is faithful; He will not let you be tempted beyond what you can bear. But when you're tempted, He will also provide a way out so that you can stand up under it* (1 Corinthians 10:13).

This passage does us no good if we are not willing to take the way of escape. Somewhere between laying down, getting naked and penetration, God provides at least one or more ways of escape. Ideally you would have taken the escape route long before you reached this point, but just in case you are hardheaded, God is gracious enough to help you out. Instead of getting frustrated because the phone rings, the smoke detector goes off, the dog starts barking, the kids start hollering or body parts don't work exactly as they should, you need to thank God for the way out of a bad situation.

Lust is always a temporary emotion and once it has been appeased, that's it. If you marry a man who physically turns you on and doesn't do anything else for you, you will be in for a rude awakening the day you realize you don't even like him, let alone love him. Lust has a tendency to make you see things that aren't really there or to overlook what is right in front of your face. Whatever you do, don't confuse lust with love:

> *Love is patient, love is kind. It does not envy, it does not boast; it is not proud. It is not rude, it is not self-seeking, it is not easily angered, it keeps no record of wrongs. Love does not delight in evil but rejoices with the truth. It always protects, always trusts, always hopes, always perseveres. Love never fails* (1 Corinthians 13:4-8a).

BREAKING UNGODLY SOUL TIES

Have you ever heard the expression "men have sex and women make love?" Basically what that means is that men and women view the act of sexual intercourse differently. Most women will not have sex without being emotionally involved on some level (which is not necessarily true for men). Once a woman has sex, a bond has been created between her and the man, regardless of whether it is a one-night stand or a long-term affair. These bonds are called soul ties. They are very serious and are very hard (but not impossible) to break.

Let me quickly make the distinction between godly and ungodly soul ties. Godly soul ties are those that occur between a husband and wife, parent and child or between friends. Naomi and Ruth's relationship is an excellent example of a godly soul tie.

God's intention was for the sexual act to occur only between a husband and a wife. The breaking of the woman's hymen indicated a blood bond (soul tie) between spouses. However, promiscuity has become rampant and because of that, each time a sexual union occurs outside the confines of marriage an ungodly soul tie is created. Don't miss this important point: *Every time a sexual union occurs outside of marriage, an ungodly soul tie is created.* If you or your intended slept with one person outside of marriage, that is one ungodly soul tie; if you or your intended slept with ten people outside of marriage, that is ten ungodly soul ties. And so on. This is serious business. The good news is there is a Bondage Breaker and ungodly soul ties can be broken:

- Ask God to forgive you.
- Ask God to reveal to you all the people with whom you have ungodly soul ties.
- Ask God to release you by praying, "Lord, in the name of Jesus, I rebuke the soul tie I have with _____." Do this for each person, one at a time. Don't worry if you can't remember names, God will know who you're talking about.
- Stand on the Word of 1 John 1:9: *"If we confess our sins, He is faithful and just and will forgive us our sins and cleanse us from all unrighteousness."*
- Confess that every soul tie is broken and the devil has no more power in this area.
- Ask God to help you to stay delivered and remember, *"...whom the Son sets free is free indeed"* (John 8:36).

You can be whole and healthy and set free from this bondage. The choice is yours.

Something to ponder...

If you have ever said, "I would never do that!" and then did exactly whatever that was, you will understand the impor-

tance of self-control. When I was growing up people used to say, "Why buy a cow if the milk is free?" What this meant was why would a man marry you if he could have all the benefits of marriage without the legal responsibility? There is a lot of truth in this simple question. Think about it. If the only reason you need a cow is for the milk, and every time you needed milk you could get it free, why endure the expense of housing, raising, feeding and caring for a cow? Not that I am calling anyone a cow, but hopefully you see the connection. It is the same principle with those who choose to experience the benefits of marriage without a wedding license. If you are going to give away what only belongs to your spouse, don't get upset if you never make it to the altar.

Questions for Reflection

1. What are some other benefits of exercising self-control?
2. Do you set yourself up and then become frustrated or do you steer clear of circumstances and people who will test your will power?
3. Ruth had a good reputation: *"...everyone in town knows you are an honorable woman"* (Ruth 3:11b). How do you think Boaz would have reacted if she had thrown herself at him instead of doing what Naomi said?
4. Are there any ungodly soul ties you need to break?

Recommended Reading

The Three Battlegrounds by Francis Frangipane
Set Apart: Discovering Personal Victory through Holiness by Bruce Wilkinson

Chapter Six
Can You Handle Responsibility?
The Power of Trust

Yes and no are some of the first words we learn; yet, they are the hardest to master because we usually say one when we mean the other. I personally get irritated with people who say they will do something and then don't. When I question them, they will say something like, "I forgot" or "I didn't mean I would really do it," which then leads to my next question: Why did you say you would? There are a lot of answers to that question: "I thought I would have the time and then found out I didn't," "I really didn't want to, but I knew you'd be upset if I said no," or "It's hard for me to say no, even when I know I can't do something."

The reality is that our lives would probably be less complicated if we would follow the advice of James 5:12b: *"Let your 'yes' be 'yes', and your 'no' no."* Although the text is talking about making oaths to God, the reminder is for all of us to become people of our word. We need to be honest with each other and ourselves. I would much rather a person said, "I don't want to do that," than to have someone say, "Sure, no problem, I'll take care of it" and then doesn't. That person then becomes unreliable, and I don't believe there is anything much worse than a person whose word doesn't mean anything. When we carelessly make promises we have no intention of keeping, that doesn't say very much about our character.

CAN GOD TRUST YOU WITH HIS STUFF?

God knew He could trust Boaz with His people, possessions and power. Boaz had already demonstrated his ability to be authoritative and master over others, and his understanding of the importance of having power and using it correctly. Most biblical commentators agree that the blessings bestowed on both the workers and Boaz by each other was a sign of a healthy employer-employee relationship: *"The Lord be with you!" he (Boaz) said. "The Lord bless you!" the harvesters replied"* (Ruth 2:4). Healthy relationships take work and do not occur overnight. Boaz treated his employees with respect, and it showed in the way they responded to him.

We don't know if he inherited the field Ruth worked in or purchased it outright, but we do know it was prosperous. Boaz wasn't a lazy man, because the Bible tells us he was in the field working and on the threshing floor winnowing barley. God knew He could trust Boaz not to forget where both his help and blessings came from.

God doesn't give us everything right away because He knows we can't always be trusted. This passage from Deuteronomy indicates that God knew forgetfulness was a distinct possibility with His children, which is why it is recorded:

> *The Lord your God will soon bring you into the land He swore to give your ancestors Abraham, Isaac and Jacob. It is a land filled with large, prosperous cities that you did not build. The houses will be richly stocked with goods you did not produce. You will draw water from cisterns you did not dig, and you will eat from vineyards and olive trees you did not plant. When you have eaten your fill in this land, be careful not to forget the Lord, who*

rescued you from slavery in the land of Egypt" (Deuteronomy 6:10-12, NLT).

CAN I TRUST YOU WITH ME?

The story of Ruth and Boaz has numerous facets: Love, faith, emotional healing, obedience and submission, but it really hinges on one thing—trust. Trust is a scary thing because you don't know what will happen until you step out in faith.

Ruth had to trust that Naomi knew what she was talking about. Have you ever had someone you trust give you bad advice? When that happens, we hesitate to receive advice from them again. Yet, at the time we thought they were correct in what they said. Even though Ruth was a foreigner from Moab, I am sure that there were parts of Naomi's plan that just didn't make sense. However, she was willing to step out in faith (trust) believing that Naomi knew what she was talking about.

Ruth also had to trust Boaz. Going to the threshing floor caused her to put her reputation on the line. She had no way of knowing how he was going to respond to her. He could have laughed at her or rejected her request and sent her off in the middle of the night.

Can't you sense the dual emotions of anticipation and anxiety inside of Ruth? She had been gleaning for approximately three months and everything had been going along fine. Then seemingly out of the blue, Naomi decided she needs to be married and came up with a plan that forced Ruth out of her comfort zone. As she was preparing for that night, she probably played various "what if" scenarios in her head. As she walked to the threshing floor, she probably encouraged herself to just get it over with. As she waited for Boaz to go to bed, you know the devil was busy telling her that this was the craziest thing she had ever done. It was bad enough leaving Moab, but at least she had Naomi. However, now she is hiding alone in the bushes waiting to ask some man to marry her! She had to be nuts. When Boaz finally went to bed, she had to wait for him to go to sleep so she could slip inside, and then she had to listen to him snore and wait for him to wake up. And all this time she is wondering what is he going to say, and although there are only two answers—yes or no—she isn't a mind reader. It is a dual set of emotions of anticipation and anxiety.

We usually hear Ruth 3:9 read the way we speak with pauses, voice inflections and so on, but I don't believe that is the way Ruth said it. After all, she had been waiting for hours to get this out, and I believe that when Boaz finally woke up and asked who she was, she blurted it all out at one time without taking a breath as if to say:

Imyourservantruthspreadthecoversofyourblanketoverme-becauseyouaremykinsmanredeemer.

Boaz then had to process what she said and she probably had to repeat it (you know how groggy you are when you first wake up). She repeated it a little slower—"I am your servant Ruth. Spread the covers of your blanket over me because you are my kinsman redeemer"—and he agreed. Now we know there was probably more dialogue than what is traditionally recorded because this was a life-changing event for both of them. I doubt very seriously if she said, "Redeem me" and he said, "Okay. Go to sleep." They probably whispered late into the night and both fell asleep with a smile on their faces. And one of Ruth's last thoughts was probably, "Naomi was right! She said just ask Boaz and he would tell me what to do and he did. I'm getting married. Wow!"

Boaz is a class act! He could have chastised Ruth for brazenly coming to him in the middle of the night, but he didn't. He had observed this woman for three months and knew that her conduct had been honorable. Matthew Henry's *Commentary of the Whole Bible* says that Boaz probably blamed himself for not having offered to be her kinsman redeemer so that she wouldn't have had to come to him. And even when he told her there was a nearer kinsman, he took care of that responsibility instead of making her ask yet another man to fulfill his obligation.

He told her to stay the night, but he made sure she was gone before anyone could discover that she had been there. Boaz knew how people liked to gossip, and he didn't want to give them any occasion to enhance their skills. Boaz also didn't want the nearer kinsman to reject Ruth because of something he assumed might have happened between Ruth and Boaz during the night. You know how people are. If they had found out about them "sleeping together," some may have wondered, "Why would she go to the threshing floor in the middle of the night?" while others would have thought, "I knew she wasn't any good, always trying to pretend like she's so humble and nice. If she's so nice, what was she doing in his bed?" Ruth had no way of knowing what Boaz would do although she was hoping he would do the right thing. Praise God, Boaz was a man of his word. He told Ruth he would talk to the nearer kinsman redeemer, and he did. The last line of Ruth 3:15 reads, *"Then Boaz returned to town"* which was after Ruth had spent the night at his feet, after he assured her he would do what she asked and after he had given her a parting gift of grain. Boaz was ready to get married and there was no reason to wait. He understood that, *"The man who finds a wife finds a treasure, and receives favor from the Lord"* (Proverbs 18:22). Boaz was already blessed by God, but he wanted the divine favor that could only come from his wife. He didn't hesitate to go back to town to talk with the nearer kinsman.

By Law the nearer kinsman had first rights to Ruth, and if he chose to execute those rights, Boaz would have to accept it. But Boaz and the nearer kinsman came to an agreement, and Boaz sent a servant to bring Ruth to him. Can you imagine how anxious she must have been? We don't know how long Boaz sat by the town gate before the nearer kinsman arrived nor how long the actual transaction took. Whether it takes five minutes or fifty, we know how it is to wait for something that is out of our control. Things were out of Ruth's hands and she could only hope for the best. She didn't know the nearer kinsman, but she knew Boaz and she was praying that somehow, some way, everything would be all right.

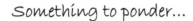

Something to ponder...

God used Boaz and Ruth to bless each other because they had their priorities straight. God knew He could trust them not to turn away or forget Him. What about you?

WAIT AND SEE WHAT HE WILL DO

When Ruth returned home, she told Naomi everything that had happened on the threshing floor and added, *"He gave me these six measures of barley, saying, 'Don't go back to your mother-in-law empty-handed.'"* Then Naomi said, *"Wait, my daughter, until you find out what happens. For the man will not rest until the matter is settled today"* (Ruth 3:16-18). Ruth had to wait because to do anything else would have been disastrous.

Now use your sanctified imagination to hear the rest of the conversation between Naomi and Ruth (Ruth's comments are italicized).

"Wait and see what he will do. Boaz is a good man and if he said he would take care of it, he will."

"Why? I did what you said. You told me it was time to find a husband and that I had to initiate the process, so I did. You told me to put on my best clothes and go down to the threshing floor, and I did. You told me to see where Boaz

slept for the night and then lay at his feet—his feet!—and I did..."

"I'm proud of you for doing what I said. I told you to rest at his feet as a sign of humility..."

"I didn't question any of the things you told me to do; although we certainly didn't have any customs like this is Moab. And now you're telling me I have to wait and see what he's going to do. What's for him to do? All he has to say is yes or no."

"I know you don't understand all of our customs and ways, but if you just trust me a little while longer, you'll see how God is going to work things out."

"Why can't I just start planning the wedding? You said he is our kinsman redeemer, and even he said he would do what I asked. Why can't I go tell everybody I'm getting married to the richest man in the area? I'm going to be Mrs. Boaz."

"Because there is a nearer redeemer who has first rights."

"I want to marry Boaz, not some stranger..."

"I know, but..."

"So why do I have to wait?"

"Because it is now up to Boaz to do what he said. Give the men time to work things out."

"But I don't want to wait!!!"

Ruth could have been disobedient and ran after Boaz to see if he had done what he said. However, she trusted Naomi's advice and realized that God didn't need any help. Waiting is hard, but necessary, and it is always rewarded.

Can't you just imagine the smile that lit Ruth's face when the servant arrived to tell her that she was wanted at the town gate? After spending time with and around Boaz, Ruth refused to believe that he would send someone else to deliver bad news. If he were going to explain why he couldn't or wouldn't marry her, he would have come himself. Ruth knew the summons was a sign that she was about to become Mrs. Boaz!

Ruth changed her clothes, combed her hair and quickly went back to town. Upon arrival she had to take a deep breath to calm down and conduct herself as the future Mrs. Boaz. She went to his side and the elders blessed their union.

How do you suppose Ruth would have felt if she kept waiting to hear back from Boaz only to discover that he never got around to speaking to the other man? That wouldn't have said very much about Boaz's character, and Ruth would have had a hard time believing any future promises he would make. It is hard to trust people who can't or won't keep their word. Because Boaz did what he said, Ruth was then able to trust him with other things, including her future.

Questions for Reflection

1. Are you trustworthy?
2. How faithful are you over what God has already given you?
3. Can God trust you not to turn your back on the things that concern Him when He blesses you with Boaz?

Recommended Reading

Having a Mary Heart in a Martha World by Joanna Weaver
Finding Favor with the King: Preparing For Your Moment in His Presence by Tommy Tenney

Chapter Seven
Walking Through An Open Door:
The Power of Destiny

When reading the book of Ruth, you will discover that all of the key people associated with this story—Naomi, Ruth and Boaz—had to put their past into perspective to walk into their destiny. They all trusted God enough to obey Him without knowing what was ahead.

Naomi moved with her husband to Moab during a time of famine in Bethlehem. The Bible doesn't tell us how long they lived there before she returned to Bethlehem, although we know it was at least ten years because that is how long Ruth was married to Mahlon. Regardless of how long, most likely Naomi had made friends and obtained some level of comfort. She followed her husband to Moab as was her duty, and followed God to Bethlehem to reach her destiny.

Ruth left her family, friends and memories to go with Naomi to a strange land. She had lived in Moab all of her life. Somewhere in her psyche she knew her destiny was intertwined with Naomi. She may not have known what to call it, but she must have felt an irresistible curiosity to be willing to leave everything she had known. She was even willing to forsake the familiar religion of idolatry to embrace Naomi's God; she trusted both Naomi and Naomi's God to take care of her.

Boaz had to be willing to put his past behind him to embrace his destiny. You may be wondering "what past?" since the Bible makes no reference to it, but are you aware that his parents were Salmon and Rahab? There is little known about his father, but his mother, Rahab, was a prostitute whose reputation for helping Joshua and the spies was legendary (Joshua 2:1-22; 6:22-26). Her story was passed down from generation to generation.

We don't get to choose our parents and some of them have done things that were embarrassing to both them and us. What do you do when your parents are the talk of the neighborhood? What do you do when everyone knows that your parents are the drunks, pimps, pushers, prostitutes and number runners? You do the same thing Boaz did: Put things in their proper perspective and move on.

There is no doubt that Boaz probably grew up being teased about his mother's former lifestyle. Regardless of her having helped the children of Israel and her embracing God, there were people around to remind others of the used to be. You know, "Didn't Rahab used to be...?" I am sure that the negative things said about his mother hurt Boaz, but somewhere along the way he decided to focus on the positive images his parents portrayed. Most boys want to grow up to be like their father, and Boaz was no different. He saw his father treating his mother with love and respect, so he did, too. I believe God created Boaz with the ability to express unconditional love for everyone, including his mother. A lesser man may have chosen to focus on the negative, but Boaz chose to focus on the positive. He refused to let his mother's former lifestyle be an excuse for him treating women in a less than respectful manner.

THE DOOR IS OPEN. WHAT ARE YOU GOING TO DO?

Remember knock-knock jokes? They were silly and sometimes made no sense at all. The whole point of a knock-knock joke was to get to the punch line, which would only come once you initially responded with, "Who's there?" You had to risk the silliness to get the prize.

It is the same with God. When God knocks on the door of our heart we respond with, "Who's there?" and instead of a silly punch line, God gives us a one-word answer: "Destiny!" In order to embrace our destiny we must open the door and then walk through it. It is risky, it is scary and at times it is unnerving because we don't know what is on the other side. Yet it is a God-ordained moment. We must believe that what is on the other side is worth having. It is a faith walk.

Naomi walked through the open door when she was willing to leave Moab and return to Bethlehem. She had to endure the "She thought she was better than everybody else and here she is right back with us" talk from the ones who stayed.

Ruth walked through the open door when she was willing to accept Naomi's God and her advice for approaching Boaz. She had to endure the "Who does she think she is?" talk from some of the other gleaners who perhaps had their eye on Boaz.

Boaz walked through the open door when he was willing to marry a foreigner and put his inheritance and reputation at risk. He had to endure the "Is he crazy? She'll take him to the cleaners! There's no way I'd marry a foreigner" talk from those who knew his status in the community.

I had to walk through the open door when I wrote and published this book. I had to step far away from my comfort zone to obey God and endure the "Are you sure you want to say that?" statements. It was harder to publish this than to write it because if it were never published, then very few people would have known that I wrote it. Publishing a book puts one in a position to be critiqued and analyzed and that is extremely uncomfortable. I did it because I knew on the other side of obedience was blessing. I also did it because it wasn't just about me. There was a woman somewhere who needed to read what God inspired me to write.

So what about you? What are you willing to let go of to embrace what God has next? The door is open, so what are you going to do? Are you going to allow your past to hinder your future or will you boldly go where no one has gone before? Don't you realize that an open door is your set-up for a blessing? Perhaps your open door is the man who is standing in front of you that you can't see because he doesn't fit your "profile." Perhaps your open door is being willing to move a relationship from acquaintance to friend-ship, from dating to courtship. Perhaps your open door is being willing to walk away from a "sure" thing. Perhaps your open door is putting fear aside and being obedient to what God has told you to do.

Only you know what doors are being opened and it is your responsibility to seek God's guidance first of all to make sure He opened the door, and then secondly to give you boldness to walk through it.

Something to ponder...

I love television, especially dramas, and one of my favorite shows is *JAG*. New episodes are no longer being produced, but I still like to watch the reruns. Two of the main characters—Harm and Sarah—had danced around a relationship for most of the series. When one was ready, the other wasn't and vice versa. Sarah was fed up with playing games and finally asked Harm, "What are you willing to give up to have me?" When I heard that line I said to myself, "That is such a great question!" Then the Lord asked me, "What are you willing to give up to have Me?" which caused me to take a serious look at some things in my life. One of the ways we "have" God is to embrace what He asks us to do and walk through open doors. So what are you willing to give up to have God in your life? Are you willing to step into your destiny? Or are you content to sit on the sidelines wishing, hoping and praying?

Questions for Reflection

1. Naomi, Ruth and Boaz had to close one door to open another. What about you? What are you willing to give up to embrace your destiny?
2. How do you feel when you hear about someone stepping into his or her destiny?

Recommended Reading

Making the Most of Your Time by Bishop Timothy J. Clarke
The Purpose-Driven Life by Rick Warren

You believe God has marriage for you, but nothing has happened yet. There is no mate on the horizon and you haven't had a date in three years, let alone someone wanting to court you! So what do you do? You wait. The Bible tells us that the promises of God are true:

> *God is not a man, that He should lie. He is not a human, that He should change His mind. Has he ever spoken and failed to act? Has He ever promised and not carried it through?* (Numbers 23:19, NLT).

If God has given you His Word on marriage, it requires patience to wait for the promise to manifest itself, especially if you see others around you being given the gift of marriage. When we find ourselves in a holding pattern, we are often tempted to jump ahead of God and make something happen, which usually results in disaster:

> *But you must not forget, dear friends, that a day is like a thousand years to the Lord, and a thousand years is like a day. The Lord isn't really being slow about His promise...* (2 Peter 3:8-9(a), NKJV).

> *...Slowly, steadily, surely, the time approaches when the vision will be fulfilled. If it seems slow, wait patiently, for it will surely take place. It will not be delayed...* (Habakkuk 2:3, NLT).

...All the days of my appointed time will I wait, till my change comes (Job 14:14, KJV)

Since ancient times no one has heard, no ear has perceived, no eye has seen any God besides you, who acts on behalf of those who wait for Him (Isaiah 64:4).

Years ago my pastor preached "A Ministry in the Meantime," which quickly became one of my favorite sermons. In this message Bishop Clarke talked about what to do between receiving a promise from God and fulfillment of the promise. I want to borrow Bishop's topic and see what Ruth can teach us about using the time between promise and fulfillment wisely.

DEVELOP AN INTIMATE RELATIONSHIP WITH GOD

Ruth was married to Mahlon for ten years. Although she was an idol worshipper during her marriage she observed Naomi worshipping God. Whatever she saw Naomi doing made her want God for herself. She was willing to leave behind everything she knew to make Naomi's God her God (Ruth 1:16b), and God was pleased with her relationship with Him. So much so that He allowed her to meet and marry Boaz and become part of the lineage of Jesus Christ.

Developing a relationship with God takes discipline. You are not ready for marriage until you have an intimate relationship with God. Someone asked me how to do that and I told them the same way you would with a man. What I mean is this: I have had several female friends push me aside when a new man came into their lives. I didn't necessarily appreciate their actions, but I understood they wanted to get to know this man by spending time with him. They weren't willing to allow anything to come between them and their new relationship. Some of the relationships worked out and some didn't, but the bottom line is they were willing to exclude every hindrance to their goal of getting to know this man.

Getting to know God is no different. Just as you set a date with a man and won't allow anything to interfere, set a date with God. Don't answer the phone, watch TV or anything else that would interfere with your date. Allow God to set the agenda and you will have the best time of your life!

An intimate relationship with God gives you that same giddy feeling you get when you are attracted to a man. You know what I'm talking about. You get excited about him calling; you smile when you think about something clever he said, you begin to find out what he likes and dislikes and so on. God gives you that same feeling in that when you have an intimate relationship with Him, you get excited about the possibility of Him speaking just to you. There is a sense of anticipation about what He is going to do next; you smile fondly when you remember something He said or did just for you and you begin to discover His likes and dislikes because you have spent time with Him.

An intimate relationship with God is key to embracing the abundant life Jesus promised. I am not necessarily speaking of material things, although you will have those. I am talking about the peace and joy that comes from being healthy and whole.

This may sound too simple, but everything doesn't have to be complicated. Trust me, this works.

EMBRACE A SPIRITUAL MENTOR

A mentor is a person who has more knowledge about a particular subject than you and is willing to share it. A mentor teaches you how to follow directions and submit to authority. Ruth recognized Naomi's maturity and wisdom even when Naomi arrived in Bethlehem and momentarily lost perspective: *"Don't call me Naomi, call me Mara."*

A mentor is not an enabler. Naomi instructed Ruth on what to do; she didn't do it for her. Naomi could have approached Boaz about fulfilling the obligation of a kinsman redeemer (see Leviticus 25:35), but Naomi picked up on the fact that there was an attraction between Ruth and Boaz and knew that Ruth had to do this for herself.

Ruth worked in Boaz's field from April until June. Every time Naomi asked, "How was your day?" Ruth probably mentioned something about Boaz. Naomi was keeping tabs on what was going on and at the right time told Ruth how to approach Boaz. Naomi recognized that Boaz was the answer to Ruth's dilemma, even though Ruth didn't seem to realize she was in one.

SOMETHING TO PONDER

When Ruth suggested to Naomi that she find work, she wasn't looking for a husband. She was doing what she needed to survive and Boaz found her working. Ruth was in the place to be blessed with a husband. We can take a lesson from her. Just do what you are supposed to do, and when it is your turn for this particular blessing, God will have your husband find you. Of course, some people want to take this to the extreme. I once had a woman tell me that she believed all she had to do was stay home and her husband would knock on her door. I am not sure what made her come to this conclusion, nor do I know how long she had been practicing this theory. I do know that she is now married and met her husband at a Christian singles' event! I am not saying to run the streets, but what are the chances of someone knock-

ing on your door saying they are God's gift to you? And in this day and age of violence would you even open the door?

LEAVE DEAD THINGS DEAD

Isaiah 43:18 says: *"Do not remember the former things, nor consider the things of old."* That is what Ruth had to do. Nowhere in the story of Ruth and Boaz do we read that she told him about her late husband, Mahlon. She had been Mrs. Mahlon for ten years and hopefully there were some good memories. Yet, when it was time to leave Moab, Ruth left all of that behind. She realized that season of her life was over. When she buried Mahlon, she buried her past.

Ruth didn't compare Mahlon and Boaz or sit around dwelling on what could have or should have been. So many women tend to get stuck in what used to be. That is not to say widows shouldn't talk about their deceased spouses and keep the good memories. I am saying that if you spend too much time dwelling on the past, you will never be able to embrace the future. The fact that you are alive makes me believe that the best is yet to come and God may possibly have another mate for you.

People who have experienced the devastation of divorce must guard against falling into bitterness. It is understandable that you are hurt and disappointed; after all, no one knowingly enters marriage with the intent of divorcing. Some women are so hurt that they shut off a part of their emotions and become bitter. When that happens you might as well crawl into the grave because you have killed a part of yourself. God doesn't want you committing emotional suicide. You were created for fellowship. When you cut off interaction with other people (especially those of the opposite sex), you miss out on God's blessings. Men and women were created to interact, not just sexually, but socially.

Single parents must also be especially careful. Please don't fall into the trap of having a pity party because you have children, or buy into the mindset that men don't want a ready-made family. If you do, you will accept a man treating you and your children like dogs just so you can say you have a man. You have to be careful about who you allow around your children and the influence they will have. Don't focus on what you don't have; instead focus on what you do have—a Heavenly Father. While God's ideal was for children to be raised in a two-parent home within the confines of marriage, I know from personal experience that He will watch over, lead and guide single parents in the raising of their children if they will let Him.

Those of you who have never married may have been involved in relationships that didn't work out quite the way you planned. Let it go. Ask God to help you glean the good part and leave the rest. My friend's father says, "Chew the meat and spit out the bones" and that is what we have to do with failed relationships. Does it hurt? Yes. Is it easier said than done? Yes. Can God bring you through without developing a spirit of unforgiveness or bitterness? Yes, if you let Him.

Don't keep regurgitating past events (and don't let other people do it for you either). Allow God to take your grief, hurt, disappointment and anger: *"Give all your worries and cares to God, for He cares about what happens to you"* (1 Peter 5:7, NLT). What do you have to lose by taking God at His Word?

TAKE CARE OF YOURSELF

Ruth was not a weakling. Gleaning was hard work and involved constant bending, stooping and working long hours in the fields. Consider how much stamina it took to be able to walk to work, work all day and then walk home carrying twenty-eight pounds of grain. Most of us get worn out carrying groceries from the car to the house!

We are not all going to wear a single digit dress size, yet we all need to find our ideal, or fighting, weight for God's work. We can't properly battle the devil and his agents if we are worn out and tired. We can't be our best for God if we don't take care of ourselves. We need to learn to eat right and find an exercise we enjoy.

All of us are busy, but constant ripping and running will wear us down regardless of our age or body size, so we need to learn the value of rest. After all, if God rested on the seventh day, why can't you? Rest is not the same as sleep. Sleep is when the powers of the body are restored; rest is freedom from activity. It took me years to learn how to rest, because I thought I had to always be doing something. I no longer try to do three, four or more things at one time and wonder why I'm still tired.

TAKE CARE OF YOUR FINANCIAL OBLIGATIONS

Ruth went to work. She recognized that she and Naomi needed money and didn't wait around for someone to take care of her or give her a hand out. She wasn't sitting around twiddling her thumbs thinking, "Woe is me, I'm just a lowly widow. Who's going to take care of me?" She went to work.

Unless you are financially independent, you probably need to work, too. Some of us make more money than we have ever dreamed and still live from paycheck to paycheck with no savings at all. Some of us are in so much debt that even if the Lord blessed us right now, we couldn't afford a wedding without setting a date a year or more in advance and then working a second job.

How is your financial health? When was the last time you had a financial checkup? Are you living within your means or are you working two jobs and still not bringing in enough income? Will you be bringing a lot of financial obligations to the marriage table?

I will confess that I have made some very unintelligent (okay, stupid!) financial decisions that caused problems in the past. I have worked very hard to eliminate those problems and be an astute steward over what God has given me. If you have ever had bill collectors call you or receive threatening mail from them, you know that it is not the most pleasant of experiences. Once I got out of financial bondage, I was determined with God's help to never repeat those same mistakes: *"Stand firm, then, and do not let yourselves be burdened again by a yoke of slavery"* (Galatians 5:1).

I want a husband who knows how to live within his means and not try to keep up with or impress other people. I will not get hooked up with a man who has an excessive amount of financial baggage (another major non-negotiable item). I expect my future husband to bring a house or car payment and maybe even a student loan. What I don't expect is multiple thousands of dollars in credit card and other debt. I am not willing to accept that, and neither should you.

There is an abundance of financial advice available and we need to take advantage of it. One of my favorite strategies is the 10-10-10-70 Percent Rule: Tithe 10 percent (give God His first), save 10 percent (because you need to have something to fall back on "just in case"), spend 10 percent on you (because you can't just pay bills and not treat yourself) and live off 70 percent (use this for all bills). Of course, depending on where you are financially, your strategy may be more 10-1-1-88 and that is okay. I don't know where I first heard about this strategy, but it does work.

Another good strategy is the debt snowball that Dave Ramsey recommends: List all of you bills, concentrate on paying off the smallest one first and then use that payment to add to the payment for the next bill. Keep doing this until all your obligations are met. Starting with the smallest bill gives you an immediate sense of accomplishment when that bill becomes history.

Just remember, it is not so much how you start as that you start. Do what you can until you can do better.

LEARN HOW TO MAKE A GOOD IMPRESSION

It has been said that you only get one chance to make a first impression. When Boaz first saw Ruth, she was working. Most likely what caught his attention was that she was new to his field, but more importantly it was that she appeared to be working hard. Boaz's foreman confirmed that she was as hard working as she appeared and Boaz was impressed. Ruth was taking care of business, not even aware that someone was watching her behavior, or that those characteristics would endear her to the man who would become her husband.

Notice also that it wasn't until *after* Boaz had some form of interaction with Ruth that he left orders for his men to leave handfuls on purpose and not to rebuke her (Ruth 2:15-16). While her looks may have attracted him, it was her demeanor that caused him to want to bless her. This order to leave handfuls on purpose was given after interacting with her over lunch. Don't miss this point, sisters. It is not enough to just look good. Something about Ruth caught Boaz's attention. Perhaps it was her knowing how to speak to him in a respectful, but not subservient manner. Perhaps it was the fact that she knew how to use the right eating utensils and chew with her mouth closed. Perhaps it was that she knew how to keep her conversation pure or that she was able to converse in an intelligent manner. Whatever it was caused him to take a second look, and in the words of comedian Arsenio Hall, made him say, "Hmm." Boaz discovered during lunch that there was more to Ruth than he had first thought.

When Naomi told Ruth to put on her best clothes to go to the threshing floor, she was telling her to make sure she looked good. We need to make sure that we are always doing what we are supposed to be doing and look good while we are doing it.

You need to discover a look that you are comfortable with and that flatters you. God made us individuals, and what looks good on one person may not look good on you. Just because something comes in your size doesn't mean you should wear it. Wear clothes that fit your body shape. Find a hairstyle that flatters your features. My hairstyle emphasizes two things about my face: my eyes and my skin. I am using what God gave me to the best advantage, and so should you. Invest in a color consultation and discover what colors look best on you. Because of my skin tone and hair color I mostly wear pink, purple or blue close to my face because brown, orange and gold don't do much for me. It is a known fact: When you look good, you feel good and you usually act the way you feel. Work with what you have until you can do better.

Something to ponder...

I once saw this absolutely gorgeous woman on the bus. Everyone—male and female—noticed her. She was physically attractive and dressed very nicely. She spoke to the bus driver, smoothed her skirt and sat down. She crossed her legs in a lady-like manner, situated her skirt again, pulled out her cell phone and then proceeded to have the most profanity-laden conversation I have ever heard in my life. And everyone—male and female—was so glad when she got off the bus. It was surprising that the women only glanced at each other, but the men were the ones talking among themselves about how much it turned them off to hear someone who looked like her talk like that. So what impression do you make?

IT DOESN'T TAKE GOD ALL DAY

If it has been a while since a promise of marriage has been given, there may be a tendency to lower the level of expectancy or anticipation. For example, if someone you care about tells you they will do something for you, there is usually an air of anticipation or excitement. However, the longer it takes for them to fulfill the promise, your expectation level lowers and you may possibly go through a range of emotion from irritated to full-blown anger. After a while, you may stop expecting fulfillment of the promise altogether. Don't get to that point. We need to keep in mind that any promise from God is already a done deal, and while it may seem like we have been waiting a long time, it really doesn't take God all day to change our situations. Consider this passage:

> As He went along, He saw a man blind from birth...He spit on the ground, made some mud with the saliva, and put it on the man's eyes. "Go," He told him, "wash in the Pool of Siloam" (this word means Sent). So the man went and washed, and came home seeing (John 9:1, 6).

There are three things about this passage to keep in mind when we talk about God's timing.

1. Jesus saw the blind man. The man didn't go looking for Jesus as Bartimaeus had.
2. During a one-sided conversation, Jesus gave him what he needed.
3. The man went from blind to sighted in the time it took to wash his face.

There are some things that you could put in place now so that when the Lord blesses you will be ready. Use this time to practice. Maybe you are like me and have to work hard on being submissive (it really isn't a dirty word!). Maybe you need to get your image together so that the "real" you can be seen in the most flattering way. Maybe you need to create and stick to a budget. Maybe you need to have a funeral for past issues. Only you know what God is saying to you. Just keep in mind that it doesn't take God all day to do something, and that one of the worst things you can do is miss His timing.

Questions for Reflection

1. How are you using the time between promise and fulfillment?
2. How is your attitude?
3. What have you been putting off?
4. Did anything in this chapter make you say "ouch" because it hit too close to home? What are you going to do about it?

Recommended Reading

To My Sisters Beloved: A trilogy of encouragement by Bishop Timothy J. Clarke
Healing for Damaged Emotions Workbook by David A. Seamands
The Gift of Forgiveness by Charles Stanley
Betrayal's Baby by P. B. Wilson
The Total Money Makeover: A Proven Plan for Financial Fitness by Dave Ramsey

Chapter Nine
It's Time For A Reality Check:
The Power of Truth

With the plethora of "reality" shows on television, it is possible for one to believe that everything you see on television is true. You have to keep in mind that for the most part television promotes fantasy. After seeking God's face for your Boaz and waiting patiently for his arrival, you don't want to fall into a "reality" mentality when it comes to marriage. I strongly believe in the concept of happily ever after; however, I also know that it takes a lot of work to accomplish.

I have talked with literally hundreds of single people over the years relating to their theories on marriage and I have discovered several myths that consistently come up during our conversations. I know there are a lot more, but based on my experience these are the top three:

MYTH NUMBER ONE:
WHEN I GET MARRIED,
I WILL HAVE FINANCIAL SECURITY.

This may or may not happen. While on the surface it makes sense that if you combine two incomes you will have more money, the reality is that with today's economy, threats of lay offs and downsizing, different spousal perceptions of what to do with the income, long-term sickness or death, two incomes may dwindle down to one. Then there is the possibility of divorce. A friend of mine calls this "shattered dreams." Christians don't go into marriage planning for divorce. There may have been extra income while married, but once divorced that additional income may dry up if there is no alimony or child support.

Another aspect to this myth is those women who believe that once they get married they will never have to work outside the home. Again, this may or may not happen. The women I know who are married to high wage earners still work to maintain their sense of independence. This is definitely something to discuss before engagement.

MYTH NUMBER TWO:
WHEN I GET MARRIED,
I CAN HAVE ALL OF THE SEX I WANT.

Yes you can, but will you? Unless you are going to masturbate, it takes two to make this happen. The reality is that in most marriages both partners work. If there are children involved, usually one parent takes on more of the burden than the other, and people do get tired. Making love every night is probably not going to happen once the honeymoon is over (if it happened then). Don't buy into the media mindset that you will make love all night long either. The reality is that a sense of lethargy comes over you after lovemaking and most people fall asleep.

Research has shown that money and sex are among the top five reasons for marital discord, so you need to be realistic when it comes to both.

MYTH NUMBER THREE:
WHEN I GET MARRIED,
WE WILL COMMUNICATE SO WELL THAT WE ARE
NOT GOING TO HAVE ANY DISAGREEMENTS,
ARGUMENTS OR HURT FEELINGS.

That is a lofty goal, but it is not realistic. People are human, prone to mistakes and your feelings are going to get hurt. It takes time to learn the rhythm—idiosyncrasies, moods, thought patterns, quirks—of another person. It doesn't happen overnight, but it will happen.

What are you bringing to the marriage table? Are you a listener or a talker? Are you organized or a pack rat? Are you task-oriented or a champion procrastinator? Do you act or react? Are you a thinker or a doer? Are you patient or impatient? Are you a loner or a people person? They say that opposites attract. If that is true, what will you face once married?

We all have different communication styles and understanding that will go a long way in avoiding misunderstandings. Perhaps your Boaz will be a less talkative person so you will need to understand that he is not upset just because he is not talking. On the other hand, you might be the less talkative person and the constant talking of your spouse may irritate you to no end.

I once overheard a conversation between a male who was a grunter and a female who was an excessive talker. The conversation started out with the male speaking full, complete sentences and slowly disintegrated to where he was using grunts to communicate. He clearly had used up his reservoir of conversation talking with this woman. When he left, I asked the woman what she thought about the conversation she just had and she said, "You know, I noticed that he started talking less and less the more I talked! And, you know what? It sort of hurt my feelings."

My point is that you need to recognize when you are dealing with a person who has a different communication style than you and make the adjustment. And don't forget, that long before you married this person you were involved in a courting relationship with them. The way they are during the courtship is usually the way they will be in marriage. Pay attention to what is going on around you.

Going into marriage expecting challenges is realistic. Going into marriage believing that everything is going to automatically work out right is a set-up for disaster.

Something to ponder...

The expression "practice makes perfect" applies to marriage. Not in the sense of multiple marriages, but in the sense of trying until you have achieved perfection in a certain area. Communication issues are also among the top five reasons for marital discord. Learning to concentrate on listening, as well as hearing, what people are saying will go a long way toward resolving marital conflict.

Questions for Reflection

1. What are your beliefs about marriage?
2. How do you feel about working after marriage?
3. What other myths can you add to the list?

Recommended Reading

An Outrageous Commitment: The 48 Vows of an Indestructible Marriage by Dr. Ronn Elmore
Saving Your Marriage Before It Starts by Les and Leslie Parrot

Chapter Ten
Wait Your Turn:
The Power of Timing

You have met the man you think may be "the one"...

You have talked on the telephone, perhaps you have exchanged numerous text messages and have probably had a few meals together...

You have tried—unsuccessfully—not to spend too much time doodling your names together inside a heart or daydreaming about "what if"...

You have started exercising and watching what you eat just in case you need to fit into a wedding dress in the near future...

You have started solidifying plans for bridesmaids, flower girls, caterers, music and all the other things associated with a wedding...

And as far as you are concerned, God can get this show on the road at any time!

God knows you are tired of being single. God knows you are ready to share your life. God knows that if you hang another bridesmaid dress in your closet or receive another wedding invitation, you are going to scream!

Don't you think God knows who you need and when you need him? Regardless to what we think or how it may appear, God is not time challenged. Philippians 4:6 says, *"Be anxious for nothing and in everything...with thanksgiving, present your requests to God."* Allow me to paraphrase that passage: "Be anxious for no thing, including marriage, and in everything give thanks for the adventure along the way."

Now, just in case you are still not convinced to let God work, I want you to remember this true story.

When I was a child, my mother worked as a professional cook, and if the era had been different she would have had the title of executive chef. I learned how to cook from her. I enjoy cooking and am quite good at it if I say so myself. I coupled my mother's teaching with a professional degree and have worked in both a commercial kitchen in a four-star hotel and as a caterer. Not long ago during a busy holiday season my schedule permitted me to take on a few catering events. I was preparing for two functions at one time because both required the same dessert: A whipped cream pound cake with a pecan and cashew crust, and yes, it tastes as good as it sounds! I needed ten cakes for both events, but I could only get four in the oven at one time, so I was *frustrated* and *tired* of waiting for the cakes to bake.

I took the last cake from the oven and it was picture perfect. It looked like something you would have seen in a food magazine. It was the perfect color; it was the perfect height, it was the perfect texture, it was just perfect! After the cake had cooled, I moved it to the plate I would give to the customer and when I lifted the cake up, a pudding-like substance oozed out. Needless to say, I was thoroughly disgusted. This cake looked done, the toothpick came out clean and it smelled wonderful. I had worked all day and cooked most of the night, so I must have imagined it was done, because when I sliced it to see what the problem was, the cake was only half-baked. Are you sensing where I am going? Whenever you get tired of waiting, I want you to remember the moral of this story:

- Everything that looks good isn't. The cake looked good, smelled good and felt good to the touch, but the appearance was deceptive.
- No matter how tired you get of waiting, or how frustrated you become, you cannot rush the process.

- If you do rush the process, you will end up repeating some steps, because tired or not you know I had to stay up to make another cake, right?

It doesn't matter how long you have been waiting. God is not slack concerning His promises. Don't jump ahead of God. God gives you certain things when He knows you can handle them. He knows what you need and when you need it. And don't forget, Boaz is alive and well and waiting for you, too!

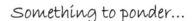

Something to ponder...

The Bible tells us that to whom much is given, much is required (Luke 12:48). Marriage is a big step and one that comes with a lot of responsibility that is not to be taken lightly. We also have the responsibility of not forgetting God when we get blessed. Do you know people who were always in church when they had a need for a new car or a job or even for a mate and then never showed back up after God blessed them? Don't let that be your testimony. Please don't disrespect God like that. We don't want to be used and discarded and neither does God.

Questions for Reflections

1. What makes you believe you are ready for marriage?
2. Do you want to be the pursued or the pursuer?

Recommended Reading

Before You Say "I Do": A Marriage Preparation Manual for Couples by H. Norman Wright et al

Conclusion: The Power Of A Testimony

Has God ever shown you something that was too big for you to wrap your arms around?

Long before salvation I imagined writing a book, but I was reluctant to start because I didn't think I would have an original idea. Because I am an avid reader, I thought I would be too influenced by the books I have read and would end up unknowingly plagiarizing someone else's concepts and words. After salvation I focused my writing skills on Sunday school lessons and workshops. When God gave me the concept for this book, I must confess I was at a place in my spiritual walk where I didn't believe He would use me in that way so I pushed the thought aside. The dream was too big. Perhaps that is something you can relate to as well.

As a child my siblings and I went to church every Sunday with our mother (my father was not saved at this time and stayed home). I enjoyed church, but I didn't understand church and just thought of it as a nice place to go on Sunday morning. I don't remember any sermons and only a few songs. My father was not a demonstrative man, so the one thing I do vividly remember about church were the hugs from my childhood pastor, the late Rev. Benjamin L. Brantley (a tall, stately, silver-haired man who stood at the back of the church every Sunday to hug and kiss the people as they left). Certainly the ministries we have in our churches today that are designed to introduce children and young people to the Lord and give them a clear understanding of biblical principles were not in evidence during my childhood. Or, if they were, I was not aware of them.

My mother battled with sickness for years and passed away when I was eighteen years old and for a number of reasons I stopped going to church. For the next several years I lived a rebellious and blatant life of sin, doing everything I thought I was grown enough to do. During that time numerous people attempted to witness to me. One of the stumbling blocks for me was that a good portion of these people were out in the streets with me doing what I was doing except they went to church on Sunday morning. But, that is not to say that I didn't hear what they were saying; I just wasn't mature enough to look past them to see Jesus.

A good friend, Deborah Thompson, received Jesus as her Lord and Savior and I saw a visible difference in her life and I respected the change. She never pressured me to get saved. She would tell me what her pastor, Bishop Timothy J. Clarke, taught during the weekly Bible study or what the sermons were about on Sunday morning, and they made sense. Whenever we would talk, she usually ended our conversations with, "Maybe one Sunday you'll come to church."

Even though I was a sinner, I have always enjoyed gospel music. One Wednesday evening in October of 1988 Deborah invited me to church for a concert. I went and had a good time. Then Deborah invited me to another Wednesday evening service the week before Thanksgiving 1988. Again, I went and had a good time. The Sunday after Thanksgiving I prepared to go to brunch at one of my favorite restaurants, but I ended up at church instead. Believe it or not, Deborah was not there (although she came in later). However, the people were very friendly. At this time the church was small, everyone knew each other and they immediately recognized that I was an outsider. They made me feel welcome and for that I will always be grateful. I have been attending First Church of God since that day.

On December 22, 1988, I accepted Jesus Christ as my Lord and Savior. I was excited and began soaking up the Word. I was falling in love with God and wanted to spend all of my time in His presence. Because I had not yet received understanding about God's sovereignty or the gifts of the Spirit or anything like that, I thought God only used preachers or "special" people and the only ministries were ushering or singing in the choir. Since ushering didn't appeal to me and while I could carry a tune there was no way I would be considered a singer, I was just glad to be saved and was perfectly content being a pew member. God had other plans.

I soon started going to the women's weekly prayer and share time. One Saturday the leader of the group (who has since gone home to be with the Lord) said, "Next week Obie's going to lead the meditation," to which I said, "No, I'm not." She said, "Yes you are," smiled sweetly and dismissed the group. I tried convincing her that day and the next that I wasn't able to fulfill this assignment, but she assured me that I could, so I finally took her at her word. What I discovered was that I enjoyed researching, studying, fasting and praying to get a specific word for a specific group of people. The Lord blessed and the women enjoyed my mini sermon. That was the beginning of my teaching ministry.

I knew that the Lord was calling me to His service, but I was unable to distinguish between whether it was a call to teach or preach (it is both), not because I was reluctant to obey, but because I couldn't understand how God would even consider using a single parent who didn't have the right credentials, pedigree or background. I didn't grow up in the church like so many others and I barely knew were Genesis chapter one was, yet God chose me as one of His messengers!

I have never had amnesia about my life of sin, and while I do not dwell on it, I do have a healthy respect for my life before Christ. I don't believe you should live in the past, but every now and then you need to stop and reflect on just how far the Lord has brought you. I was teaching a class once and shared part of my testimony. After the class, one of the participants cautioned me about sharing so much because people didn't need to know. While there was some truth in what this person said, a part of the problem with the Church today is we don't want to share our story. We are to encourage one another and we do that by letting people know where we have come from. One of the benefits of staying in a close relationship with God is His telling you what to say, when to say it and how much to share. There is a time and place for everything, and you need to remember that everything you have been through has been so you can bless someone else by telling them, "If I survived, so can you. God will bring you through."

Once I accepted God's love, forgiveness and mercy, I was able to start walking into the destiny He has prepared for me. One Sunday morning I was sitting in the service and Bishop was preaching. Suddenly the title of this book popped in my head, and I wrote it on the edge of my bulletin and re-focused on the service. Later that night the Lord brought the title back to my mind, and I asked Him what was I supposed to do with it? He said, "Write a book," to which I said the equivalent of "Yeah, right. Me write a book about Boaz," and didn't think any more about it. It was about six months later that the Lord brought the title back to me again and I began outlining chapters, although it would still be three years before I completed the project.

You might be wondering why I didn't immediately pull out paper and pen to begin writing when the Lord gave me this title. Well, that is a long story (and another book). Suffice it to say, the Lord took me on a wilderness journey to introduce me to me and to show me His love. As I got closer to the Promised Land, I began the labor pains of this book. There were times when the words flowed fluently. There were also times when I felt as if I needed to push and nothing happened! I had no idea how long the book would be or exactly what I would write. The Lord told me not to worry about the end before the beginning, so I didn't concern myself with whether anyone would publish the book, purchase the book or read the book. I knew I had to write it and that God would take care of the rest.

Once the book was finished and it had been read by my critique group and revised numerous times, *Waiting for Boaz* was finally ready. I then started investigating how to get the book published and researched the most economical way to maintain control over the product I had prayed and fasted to produce. I knew approximately how much money it would take and told the Lord He would have to find it for me. I had no way of knowing that the way He would use would involve a car accident and an insurance payoff, but it did.

One Sunday afternoon my son took my car back to school in Pennsylvania because he was coming home again the following weekend (I was home recuperating from knee surgery and hadn't yet been released to resume driving). My son called me a few hours after leaving to tell me he had been in an accident, but that he was okay although he was going to the emergency room as a precaution. He called back about an hour later to let me know the damage to the car, which was extensive on the passenger side. A car had run him off the road outside of Cleveland, Ohio and while trying to get control, he and the other drivers hit a patch of black ice and started spinning. My son ran into a guardrail on the passenger side and a semi truck sideswiped the driver's side. The car that started the whole mess kept going.

I called the insurance company to start the process of having the car repaired. They informed me that the repairs exceeded the value of the car and they were going to total it. Initially, I wasn't happy about that because my car was paid for, but once I calmed down I realized this was a blessing from God. The money from the insurance company allowed me to buy a used car for myself, buy a used car for my son (so he could stop driving mine!) and publish this book. When I realized what God had done and how He had done it, all I could do was laugh. You do know that God has a sense of humor, right? God is too good to be boxed into a certain way of doing things and when we allow Him to work He demonstrates that He is very creative. Isn't God good?

This entire writing experience has taught me how to trust God more. I have learned how to seek His face for the boldness to do and say what He wants. It has also given me a deeper love for His people, especially His women.

My sister, I have prayed for you throughout this writing process so that you will be able to receive what the Lord has in store for you. Please wait for what God has for you, no matter how long it takes. When God makes a promise, it is better than anything else, and at His appointed time it will come to pass.

> May the Lord bless and protect you.
> May the Lord smile on you
> and be gracious to you.
> And may the Lord show you His favor
> and give you His peace.
>
> Numbers 6:24-26 (NLT)

Recommended Reading

The Dream Giver by Bruce Wilkinson.

Afterword: Why We Need A Kinsman Redeemer

In biblical times a kinsman redeemer was the one who was willing to do for someone what they couldn't do for themselves. In order to fulfill the obligation, the kinsman redeemer had to meet the following criteria: He must be the near of kin; he must be able to redeem (and be free of needing redemption himself) and he must be willing to redeem.

Jesus Christ is our great Kinsman Redeemer because He meets all of the criteria and is the only one able to save us. He chose to come to earth to redeem His people. If you have never asked Him into your life, now is the time to do so. The Bible says, *"Today if you hear my voice, do not harden your heart"* (Hebrews 3:15, NKJV). God wants to have a relationship with you, and you will never be all that He intends without Him in your life. If you are ready to ask the Lord into your life, pray this prayer:

> Father, please forgive me for all the times I have tried to do things my way instead of yours. I confess that I am a sinner and I cannot save myself. I believe that Jesus Christ is your Son who died on the cross in my place. I believe that He rose on the third day and ascended into heaven where He sits at your right hand. I believe He is coming back again. Please come into my heart and cleanse me from all sin and unrighteousness. Please fill me with the precious Holy Spirit. From this day forward I belong to you, and I accept you as my Lord and Savior. In Jesus' name. Amen.

Once you have prayed this, you are saved. Don't worry about whether you "feel" saved or not. The Word of God says, *"That if you confess with your mouth, 'Jesus is Lord,' and believe in your heart that God raised Him from the dead, you will be saved"* (Romans 10:9). There are three things you need to do:

1. Tell somebody the good news that you are saved. The Bible tells us that angels in heaven rejoice over one sinner coming to repentance. E-mail me at obierogers@aol.com and let me share in the celebration.

2. Find a church home where the Bible is being preached and taught.

3. The Bible is God's instruction book so you need to be able to read the manual to know what God expects from you. Find a translation of the Bible you can understand and read it regularly.

You have made the best decision of your life. Accepting Jesus as Lord and Savior doesn't mean you won't have any more problems, because you will. But it does mean that you have Someone to help you with your problems. God bless you.

Please enjoy this excerpt from *On The Other Side of Yes: Understanding the Power of Agreement*

INTRODUCTION

Have you ever read something that kept you thinking about the subject long after you finished? Something that was so enlightening that it caused you to re-examine your thinking or behavior? It doesn't happen often, but when it does, all you can say is, "Wow!"

I had often heard, and had even quoted, Amos 3:3 (KJV), *"Can two walk together, except they be agreed,"* but it wasn't until I read a magazine article in my doctor's waiting room that I understood what the Scripture meant. I don't remember the name of the magazine or who wrote the article; I just remember the content: Entering into agreement with someone of the same mindset will manifest itself in a powerful way.

The article I am referring to was written by a married couple chronicling the story of their son who was born with a congenital illness. The doctors advised the parents to terminate the pregnancy. They listened to the doctor's reasoning for termination, and after extensive prayer, decided to have the baby. The parents didn't know everything the child would face, but knew that whatever was ahead would be demanding and involve long hospital stays and multiple operations. They chose to proceed in faith. The parents committed to be in total agreement about their child's treatment before he was born and were at peace because they agreed they were doing what they believed to be best.

Once the child was born he did face daunting physical challenges. Despite all of that, the parents were always in agreement about their child's treatment, even when it went against the doctors' recommendations. That is not to say that they didn't esteem the doctors, because they had confidence in their training; however, it is to say that this couple had their faith in the Great Physician and every step of the way they were seeking God for guidance.

After reading the article, I began to study how important and powerful agreement actually is. This book is a result of my research and I have discovered three essential truths:

- You can agree with yourself: Will you eat another piece of cake or go for a walk? Will you spend your last dollar to play the lottery or save it toward paying your bills? Will you spend more time in the Word or continue wasting time doing other things that are less important?

- You can agree with someone else: Will you loan someone money until payday or will you participate in an armed bank robbery? Will you go to Bible study or to happy hour with your friends?

- And you can agree with God: This one is a little more challenging, because if things don't work out the way you want—unlike agreeing with yourself or someone else where you can blame someone or some thing if it doesn't work out—you can't blame God. He is perfect, which means that whatever you agreed with Him to do is perfect, too. You have to accept the outcome and believe that things worked out the way they were supposed to, even if you don't like the way they worked out.

A MARRIAGE MADE IN HEAVEN

The greatest tool in the Christian's arsenal is the power of the Holy Spirit and all that He brings with Him when we say yes to His coming into our lives. Sometimes we take for granted just how much power the Holy Spirit endows us with when we accept Jesus Christ as our Lord and Savior.

The Bible tells us that, *"The tongue has the power of life and death"* (Proverbs 18:21, NIV) and we know that we should, *"Simply let your 'Yes' be 'Yes,', and your 'No' be 'No'"* (Matthew 5:37, NIV), but I often wonder if we really understand just how much power we have when two or more of us come into agreement:

> *Take this most seriously: A yes on earth is a yes in heaven; a no on earth is no in heaven. What you say to one another is eternal. I mean this. When two of you get together on anything at all on earth and make a prayer of it, my Father in heaven goes into action. And when two or three of you are together because of me, you can be sure that I'll be there* (Matthew 18:19, The Message).

The importance of intercessory prayer cannot be minimized, and one of the best places to practice the power of agreement is during corporate worship. There is not a person saved today who hasn't benefited from someone standing in the gap for them. We need to agree with the intercessor, whether we like their style of praying or not. Some intercessors are very loud (almost as if they believe God is deaf!) while others are very soft-spoken. Yet, all have the ability to touch heaven, and so do we when we line up in agreement with them.

We can also practice the power of agreement during the sermon. The man or woman of God who is bringing forth the Word has already studied and prepared. We can make their delivery easier by agreeing with them before, during and after the preaching.

A final place to practice agreement is during the altar call. Can you imagine what would happen if every believer got into agreement with what God does during the altar call? That is not the time for you to tip out so you can beat the traffic or take a potty break. Lives and souls are at stake, and one day it may be your family member fighting for domination of their soul. Which would you prefer: Someone agreeing with the man or woman of God or someone who just had to leave for no reason other than not wanting to sit in line to get out of the parking lot?

SO WHAT'S THE BIG DEAL ABOUT AGREEMENT?

On the Other Side of Yes: Understanding the Power of Agreement contains what I believe to be the ideal biblical illustrations of diverse types of agreements. Regardless of whether you are in complete accord or involved in an agreement because of someone else's decision, there is no turning back once a yes response has been given.

The big deal about agreements is that they are powerful and permanent. You cannot undo the events that are set in motion, whether good or bad, when you join in agreement. And, because they are so powerful and permanent, you must be careful about the agreements you make.

Throughout this book you will discover that agreements can be positive and negative, potent and dangerous, rewarding and fulfilling. You will be reminded that *who* you agree with is just as important as *what* you are agreeing on, and that whether you agree by saying yes, okay, uh-huh, nodding your head, grunting, moaning or remaining silent, the principle of Amos 3:3 remains the same: *"Can two walk together, except they be agreed?"*

Other books by Obieray Rogers

On the Other Side of Yes:
Understanding the Power of Agreement
ISBN 978-14664224-1-6

The Heaven on Earth Trilogy (fiction)

Book One—*A Hug From Daddy*
ISBN 978-0-9764022-2-0

Book Two—*The Wonder of Love*
ISBN 978-14495628-9-2

Book Three—*Kiss Yesterday Goodbye*
ISBN 978-14664224-1-4
Available February 2012

WWW.OBIEROGERS.COM
A fresh voice in Christian fiction and inspiration.

Made in the USA
Columbia, SC
16 October 2020